TECH SPEAK

or
HOW TO TALK HIGH TECH

An Advanced Post-Vernacular Discourse
Modulation Protocol

TECH SPEAK

or
HOW TO TALK HIGH TECH

EDWARD TENNER

CROWN PUBLISHERS, INC.
NEW YORK

Published by Crown Publishers, Inc.,
225 Park Avenue South,
New York, New York 10003
and represented in Canada by the Canadian MANDA Group
CROWN is a trademark of Crown Publishers, Inc.
Manufactured in the United States of America
Library of Congress Cataloging-in-Publication Data
Tenner, Edward.
    Tech speak.
    Includes index.
    1. Vocabulary.   2. English language—Technical
English.   3. Words, New—English.3 I. Title.
PE1449.T46   1986   428.1   86-986
ISBN 0-517-56220-0
10 9 8 7 6 5 4 3 2 1
First Edition

CONFIGURATION

ACKNOWLEDGMENTS

For advice and encouragement I am grateful to Drs. Dwight Bolinger, Enoch Durbin, David McNeill, Michael Silverstein, Janice Moulton, William Robinson, Geoffrey Nunberg, Thomas McMahon, Arthur Winfree, Stephen Morse; to my colleagues at Princeton University Press, especially Charles Creesy, Deirdre Sheean, Trudy Glucksberg, Barb Stump, Florence Slade, Margaret Rosso, Marjorie Sherwood, and Robert Brown; and to Landon Y. Jones, Roy Mottahedeh, Susan Milmoe, and Richard Woodbridge. I am also indebted to my editor, Lisa Healy, for her invaluable help in getting from idea to book.

A note on the illustrations: Illustrations on pages 21, 27, 33, 41, 49, and 53 are by Freelance Associates Inc., special thanks to Joseph Dougherty. All others are by Bohdan Osyczka.

PREFACE

Some people believe that English is in trouble. Bill Moyers of CBS News has called on the graduating class of the Lyndon B. Johnson School of Public Affairs to join the "guerrilla war against the pollution of our public language," a threat that "contaminates the body politic as surely as tainted meat poisons the human body."

Language scholars are more restrained in condemning jargon. Marie Borroff, the William Lampson Professor of English at Yale and teacher of its undergraduate course in the history of the English language, has defined Techspeak (her spelling) as "writing that presents its subject matter, at an advanced educational level, in terms of a set of ideas." She considers it necessary within limits but advises against using too many "Latinate" words.

I share Mr. Moyers's and Professor Borroff's love of plain English. But I can't agree with some critics that our language needs saving. It has often been flooded with new, pretentious words. It has survived them. Nasty people sometimes use clever expressions to cover their tracks, but this has always been a bad strategy for them. Fancy talk calls attention to itself. The best vocabulary for evildoing is silence.

When I started to write this book, I looked for scholars and scientists studying how technical language originates and spreads. I was surprised by how few there are. Jargon is one of the liveliest sources of our speech, as the styles of Church and Court once were. It is often unintentionally hilarious, and we should laugh at it. But it also has a profound side, and we should take it seriously. I hope this book helps readers do both.

In this spirit, I have written *Tech Speak* to help consumers of new words become producers. It can pay. For example, having once studied and taught history, I know that this discipline's venerable name discourages some prospective pupils and nonacademic employers. Isn't *history* what Voltaire wrote at the court of Frederick the Great? Some now call their profession *cliometrics*—a step in the right direction, worthy of its cousin disciplines, *demographics* and *psychonomics.* For the historian, Tech Speak suggests *interpretive long-term file linkage, retrodictive sociocultural dynamics,* or (my favorite) *holistic diachronic analysis.*

Tech Speak can help in politics, too. Liberals are unpopular. Tech Speak can help them become Neoliberals. Liberals build schools and roads. Neoliberals develop human capital and the infrastructure.

To help you get started, I look at how Tech Speak came about, give more than two dozen case studies, present a procedure for assembling Texpressions (as we call Tech Speak's compound words), and let you practice on your own. In case anybody is still unambiguous about jargon after finishing this book, I've added a Nontechnical Epilogue with some reflections on the subject—in Vernacular English.

A TECH-SPEAK CHRONOLOGY

1066   Norman Conquest. The dawn of legalese, leading to *assizes of novel disseisin, escheats, forme-
dons, easements, reversions, chattels,* and other
bulwarks of our liberty.

1382   First attested use of *input* (to mean to contribute)
in Wycliffe's translation of the Bible.

ca. 1450   Secular humanism is invented. Professional
family names are changed to Greek and Latin
(Schwarzerd to Melanchthon, Bauer to Agri-
cola).

1610   First attested use of *dichotomy,* in a translation of
The City of God: "This Trichotomy . . . doth not
contradict the other Dichotomy that includeth
all in action and contemplation."

1693   First attested use of *structure* as a verb, in a
translation of Rabelais: " . . . Equity and Justice
being structured and founded on either of the
opposite terms. . . ."

1735   Linnaeus publishes *Systema Naturae,* founding
uniform scientific classification.

1

1755   Samuel Johnson's *Dictionary* defines a network as "any thing reticulated or decussated, at equal distances, with interstices between the intersections."

1761   Linnaeus is given a patent of nobility for his Latin classification; his name is de-Latinized to von Linné.

1798   First attested use of *modular,* in a mathematics book's reference to "the greatest load which a modular wall, or column, could carry."

1802   Jeremy Bentham coins *minimize* (to be done to evil) and *maximize* (to be done to an "appropriate moral aptitude," among other things) in his *Principles of Judicial Procedure.*

1858   First attested use of *output,* as an ironmasters' expression for the quantity of metal produced.

1859   First attested use of *parameter* outside mathematics, in a book on optics referring to the index of refraction between two media.

1882   *Deconstruction* appears for the first time in English, in a historian's description of "a reform the beginnings of which must be a work of deconstruction."

1926   General Jan Christian Smuts coins *holism* in his book *Holism and Evolution.*

1944   *American Speech* notes an early nonchemical use of the word *catalyst.*

1945   The Allies win World War II. German rocket scientists are brought to the United States, promoting nominal compounds.

1946   George Orwell publishes "Politics and the English Language," arguing that foolish thoughts have not only brought about slovenly language, but have resulted from it as well.

1960   *Acronyms, Initialisms, and Abbreviations Dictionary* is issued, with 12,000 entries.

1966   David McNeill, a psycholinguist, discovers the spread of noun compounds from space engineering; congressmen score higher on an oral "pomposity index" than NASA engineers. (The longest known nominal compound had appeared in the *Congressional Record: liquid oxygen liquid hydrogen rocket powered single stage to orbit reversible boost system.*)

ca. 1968   Zbigniew Brzezinski coins *technetronic*.

1971   John B. Connally calls controls "parameters"; first attested official use.

1972   The Nixon Administration decrees that all presidential orders and agency rules are to be written in "laymen's terms."

1974   The *Federal Register* (according to *Newsweek*) announces a new position in the State Department to "review existing mechanisms of consumer input, thruput and output."

1975   R. Buckminster Fuller, with E. J. Applewhite, publishes *Synergetics,* the *Ulysses* of Tech Speak.

1977   The Carter Administration orders department and agency heads to use "plain English" in official announcements.

1979   A U.S. Labor Department press release calls truckdrivers "transport equipment operatives."

1980   President Carter describes plans to "strengthen linkages among macro-economic, sectoral place-oriented economies."

1981   Alexander M. Haig, Jr., is appointed U.S. Secretary of State.

1984   U.S. delegates to a London economic summit meeting introduce *derigidification, flexibilization,* and *restructuralization.*

1985   A new edition of the *Acronyms, Initialisms, and Abbreviations Dictionary* is published, with over 300,000 entries.

           (For the latest in attested Tech Speak, see the National Council of Teachers of English *Quarterly Review of Doublespeak,* which originally reported a number of the items above.)

INTRODUCTION:
Join the Jargonauts

For decades—in fact, for centuries—hundreds of thousands of professionals have been at work on a new release of the English language. From physicians to aerospace engineers, from public officials to food packagers, they have scrutinized every word, including some unchanged since the days of Alfred the Great, and have made vast improvements reflecting our knowledge of matter, energy, life, and society. It is time to begin disseminating their work: Tech Speak.

Tech Speak consists of jargon, but it's more than jargon. It unifies rather than separates people, as jargon does. It has all the advantages of medieval Latin without those confusing inflections. If you asked Tech Speak to define itself, it would probably say something like this:

> Tech Speak is a postcolloquial discourse modulation protocol for user status enhancement. It's a referential system for functional-structural, microscopically specific macroscopic-object redesignation. It's a universal semantic transformation procedure. It's a holophrastic technocratic sociolect. It's a meta-semiotic mode for task-specific nomenclature.
>
> Tech Speak is an accretive substantive-compound formulation tool. It's a representational Newtonian-solid identification technique. It's an n-dimensional matrix of

analytical denomination-conventions. It's a recombinant autonomous neologistic paradigm. It's a post-Linnaean taxonomic organic/inorganic classificatory strategy.

Tech Speak is an advanced quasi-denotative anthropoid communication system. It's a global lexical reconstruction convention. It's a personal-database enrichment project. It's a self-referential meta-dialect.

Tech Speak is a secular hieratic neologistic deference induction methodology. It's a modular, military/industrial-strength phrasal concatenation routine. It's an agglutinative nonlocalized terminological corpus. It's a comprehensive normative locution inventory.

Tech Speak is a syncretic Greco-Latinized post-industrial interlanguage. It's a device-mediated spontaneous sociolinguistic mutation. It's a value-neutral, ahistoric, non-connotational, affect-free, metaphrastic message-transmission medium with unique intersubjective symbolic-interactive capabilities.

Just as Tech Speak may have dozens of ways to say the same thing—like Vernacular English—it has equal numbers of things to call itself. To present this advanced semiotic mode, here is a cognitive input device in the form of a randomly accessible instantaneous-readout pre-formatted information-retrieval batch-processed pigment-saturated gathered-signature laminous-cellulose hardcopy output matrix. This graphically augmented extended alphanumeric string will enable readers to access the discourse production subroutines of defense subcontractors, decipher the pseudepigrapha of psychiatrists, penetrate the proleptic prose of professors, and assimilate the sibylline polysyllables of civil servants—all of whom have been generating contextually segregated Tech Speak components for decades. Each part of Tech Speak has seemed forbidding and mystifying. Understood as a whole, it is enlightening and liberating.

It enlightens by revealing the wonder and complexity of things we take for granted. It liberates by lifting the barrier between expert and layperson—an obstacle that plain-language movements have never been able to budge.

What Tech Speak Isn't

Tech Speak isn't simply pompous or euphemistic talk. People have tried for centuries to impress one another with long and exotic words, but only functional/structural accuracy makes pretension Tech Speak.

Barbers used to call themselves "tonsorial artists" and their shops "tonsorial emporiums" or "salons." This wasn't Tech Speak. A correct self-description would have been *keratin management professionals* and *keratin management facilities,* respectively. (Today cosmetics is one of Tech Speak's showcases, with *RNA bio-complexes, electro-bond proteins, hypoallergenics,* and *technician-operated individualized diagnostic systems.*)

In proper Tech Speak, a "memorial park" is a *biolysis center,* and a "thanatologist" is a *nonviable somatic transition specialist.* A "beverage host," "beverage attendant," or "mixologist" (perhaps "beverage consultant," soon) is an *applied ethanol chemist.* The reputed Congressional "footwear maintenance engineer" is a *propulsive interface technician.* A "turf accountant" is an *equine concurrent bioenergetic evaluation professional.*

Only the schools seem to get these matters right. There are still institutions, I am told, where time is measured in *instructional modules* and pupils brought to and fro in *motorized transportation modules.*

Tech Speak is not the language of scientists and engineers. Technical and scientific people have been the most

7

important contributors to Tech Speak, but it isn't their every-day dialect. Of course, there are papers in which acid rain appears as "atmospheric deposition of anthropogenically derived acidic substances," but scientists don't talk that way to each other. They use a professional dialect mixing technical words, technical slang, and Vernacular English. For instance, elementary-particle physicists like to use whimsical words even for advanced concepts, such as the "color," "charm," and "flavor" of quarks.

Finally, Tech Speak is not merely a series of long words. Just as some elaborate expressions don't qualify as Tech Speak, some simple ones do. Short, everyday words may be impeccable Tech Speak, *as long as they are not used in their Vernacular English senses.* A *plate* or a *dish* may be almost anything but a ceramic nutrient-manipulation surface. A *pod* may contain anything but vegetable germinal material. A *seal* should not be a pinniped; *ports* and *anchors* are not for aquatic transport vehicles, nor is a *buffer* used on dactylic keratin; a *sink* is not for liquid processing, a *cell* for felons, *booting* for pressurized agonistic projectiles, or an *icon* for veneration.

The Mysterious Familiar

This book starts with the everyday, not because it is the easiest aspect of the world to learn, but because much of it is the most difficult. Ordinary things sometimes have been understood only after cosmological and atomic processes were known. Not until the 1940s did we start to learn how friction works. The motions of a falling leaf, the formation of snowflakes, and the glint of sunlight on the waves need mathematical models more complex than those describing planetary orbits. Although humanity has used cement ever since the ancient Egyptians invented it, and now produces a billion tons of it each year, researchers still can't agree about how it combines with water. In fact, wetting, tearing, and freezing are also at the frontier of knowledge. We have learned more about some rare primates than about the feeding habits of backyard squirrels. Even household pets are more complicated than we think; cats need twenty-two amino acids—more than people do.

If you think plain English is easy, try talking to a computer with it. Only the boldest of scientists are trying to model *fuzzy discourse,* as our daily speech is called in artificial-intelligence circles. "Expert systems" can make the most refined diagnoses of complex diseases (though one meningitis-diagnosis program, according to *The Economist,* can say of a corpse only that it does not have meningitis), but can't cope with the mental world of an average schoolboy. Building a robot with the visual-discrimination ability of a pigeon will be a triumph.

Tech Speak brings rigorous structural-functional description to this terrifyingly complex set of phenomena we call daily life, whether in a *nutrient preparation zone* (NPZ) or an *intergenerational information transfer environment* (IITE). Far from threatening civilized English with barbarism, as critics charge, it replaces the jargon of Indo-European herdsmen and medieval shopkeepers with expressions that correspond as closely as possible to the working of the things they signify.

You can name and describe anything in Tech Speak. You need only talk about it as though you had just invented it. By setting aside all the connotations of a familiar word and introducing others, the Tech Speaker is almost creating a new thing. For example, anything large enough to be visible is, in Tech Speak, a *macroscopic object* (MO). Since people spend most of their time dealing with MOs (including other people), this book begins with a series of MOs and MO-*complexes* (MOCs), which are simply MOs often found in association. These are only a beginning. You will discover powerful Tech-Speak expressions of your own for the same items. Of course, there are thousands of other MOs awaiting definition.

To help you be your own Texicographer, there's a second section with a *nominal compound generation algorithm*—a set of procedures for making new Tech-Speak expressions. There is no Tech-Speak Academy. There is no single correct Tech-Speak word for anything. No word would be long enough. Each Texpression reveals a different use or feature of some macroscopic object or institution. Like the words of other languages, some are more elegant than others, but each is best for some time and place. Tech Speak is an invitation to discover as many Texpressions as possible. Although Tech Speak is not a religion, it does have its own formulation of the Meaning of Life: *participant empirical data generation* (PEDG).

Finally, to start you on your way as a Tech Speaker, there is a series of pre-labeled macroscopic objects, past as well as present. Tech Speak is not only for new MOs, but for retrofitting to old ones.

This book is written mostly in Vernacular English. Simplified Tech Speak does not work because Tech Speak must use complexity up to the limit of our comprehension to reveal the intricate true nature of the things it represents. Of course, it never achieves this. It is always an incomplete account of our imperfect knowledge. While Vernacular English may seem lucid and Tech Speak opaque, that is only because we don't bother to think about the origins of Vernacular English words. If we did, we would find that many are based on philosophical and social theories much stranger than the ones underlying Tech Speak. But they still help us to understand Tech Speak, and we are likely to be bilingual for a long time.

Even embedding Tech Speak in Vernacular English may not clarify all Tech Speak words illustrated here. Questions are natural. Fortunately, Tech Speak has already found its way into many larger standard reference books, some of which are listed in the Hard-Copy Module Directory at the end of this volume. If you keep a notebook of the Texpressions that you find and invent, your vocabulary and generative skill will thrive.

A PICTORIAL TEXICON

Empirical research suggests that anthropogenic macro-scopic object juxtaposition is a nonrandom psychoso-cial process. To operationalize this hypothesis, a free-association-generated set of macroscopic objects was collated for high-resolution monochromatic two-dimensional representation with definitional peripheral Tech-Speak copy in both articulated-ostensive and dis-cursive-textual modes. Tech-Speak Notes document Texpression implementation.

Organisms are microscopic or macroscopic reduced-entropy carbon-rich dynamic systems. More precisely, they are viable Phanerozoic biomass constituents: en-vironmentally adapted, osmotically pressurized, homeo-static multicellular eukaryotic protoplasmic terrestrial, airborne, and aquatic macromolecular assemblies, cap-able of symbiotic nondirected multigenerational genetic self-engineering through selective pressures on products of mutationally semi-randomized chromosomal recombinant iterations.

(In certain North American jurisdictions, organisms may instead replicate antediluvian canonical, omnipotently/providentially established, paleographically document-ed discrete morphogenetic prototypes.)

The **chromatic pollination motivator** (CPM) is an angiosperm reproductive module for arthropod-mediated intraspecific fertilization. This composite variety, though anthropogenically propagated, optimizes apian transfer through flavonoid pigmentation.

Tech-Speak Note

In his essay "Politics and the English Language" (1946), George Orwell observed that *antirrhinium* was starting to replace *snapdragon,* and *myosotis* was being preferred to *forget-me-not.* Orwell detected "an instinctive turning away from the more homely word."

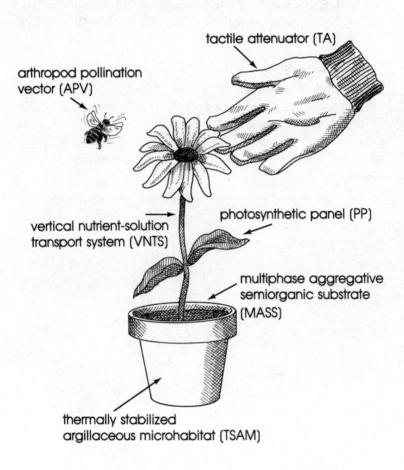

tactile attenuator (TA)

arthropod pollination vector (APV)

vertical nutrient-solution transport system (VNTS)

photosynthetic panel (PP)

multiphase aggregative semiorganic substrate (MASS)

thermally stabilized argillaceous microhabitat (TSAM)

Chromatic Pollination Motivator

Shown here in nurturant phase, the **in vivo recombinant genetic system** (IVRGS) is a dyadic hominid autopropagation unit for intergenerational meiotic chromosome redistribution.

Tech-Speak Note

The best Tech-Speak definition of IVRGS constituents to date is that given by the anatomist L. A. Borradaile in 1912: "metazoan, triploblastic, chordate, vertebrate, pentadactyle, mammalian, eutherian, primate" (cited in Theodore H. Savory, *The Language of Science* [London: A. Deutsch, 1953], 19).

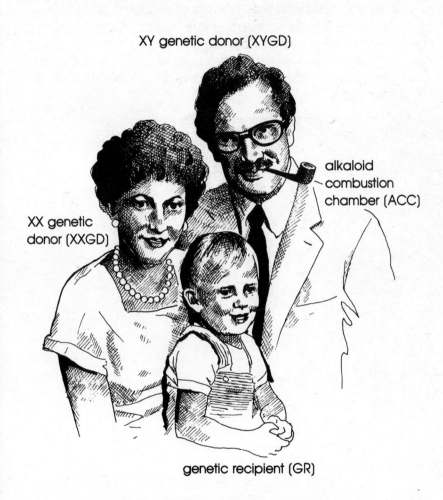

XY genetic donor (XYGD)

alkaloid combustion chamber (ACC)

XX genetic donor (XXGD)

genetic recipient (GR)

In Vivo Recombinant Genetic System

The **stochastic technician** (ST) operates voluntary aleatory interpersonal contractual randomized resource-entitlement redistribution systems, reallocating proprietary dedicated polymeric credit vouchers (DPCVs) to reflect probabilistically weighted outcomes of initial-state-dependent unpredictable discrete-state Newtonian processes.

luminous energy baffle (LEB)

polymeric credit vouchers (PCV)

hexahedral random digit generators (HRDG)

Stochastic Technician

Nutrient systems (NS) are trophic objects and physico-chemical apparatus, including cultivar-, botanical-, arthropod-, piscine-, avian-, ruminant- (and other ungulate-) derived mono-, di-, and triglycerides, di- and polysaccharides, and peptide-bonded amino acids. These lithosphere- and hydrosphere-derived, unprocessed or chemosynthesized hydrocarbon-rich energy, alkaloid, and mineral sources, in conjunction with the vitrified kaolin, fused-silicate, and ferrous and non-ferrous thermoregulatory, microbial, and reactive apparatus and ingestive modalities for alimentary canal introduction and uptake, support anthropoid motor, nervous, cortical, and cerebral function.

The **dual carbohydrate-oxidation chamber** (DCOC) is an electroresistive self-limiting Maillard reaction initiator for infrared irradiative thermal preparation of microbially aerated, kiln-stabilized milled cereal-endosperm sections for accelerated absorption of spatula-delivered nonfermented bovine lipid emulsions or hydrogenated carotene-pigmented vegetable glycerides.

Tech-Speak Note

The ingredients of one popular brand of "natural" carbohydrate sections include (among others): mono- and diglycerides, ethoxylated mono- and diglycerides, potassium bromate, monocalcium phosphate, calcium sulfate, ammonium sulfate, and ferrous sulfate.

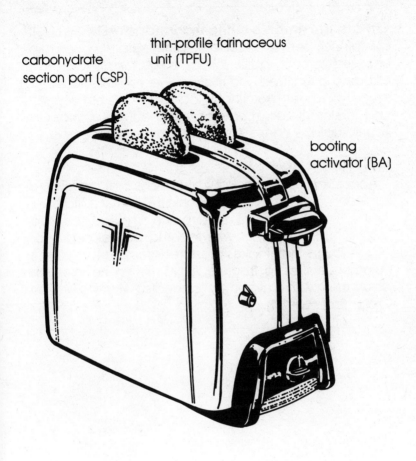

carbohydrate
section port (CSP)

thin-profile farinaceous
unit (TPFU)

booting
activator (BA)

Dual Carbohydrate-Oxidation Chamber

The **avian embryo nutrient cartridge** (AENC) is a self-contained, semi-permeable, biomineralized-calcium-encased osmotic gallinaceous epigenetic environment capable in fertilized and maternal- or radiant-incubated mode of full-term ornithological development support, and in unfertilized mode of interspecific (anthropoid) trophic uptake after thermal/mechanical processing.

Tech-Speak Note

According to Gene Haugh, professor of agricultural engineering at Virginia Polytechnic Institute and State University, the AENC is like an airplane fuselage or a submarine hull: a cylinder with tapered and closed ends. Haugh found that it takes pressures greater than those in automobile tires to fracture AENCs when he injection-tested them with a hypodermic needle (*Washington Post,* September 9, 1984).

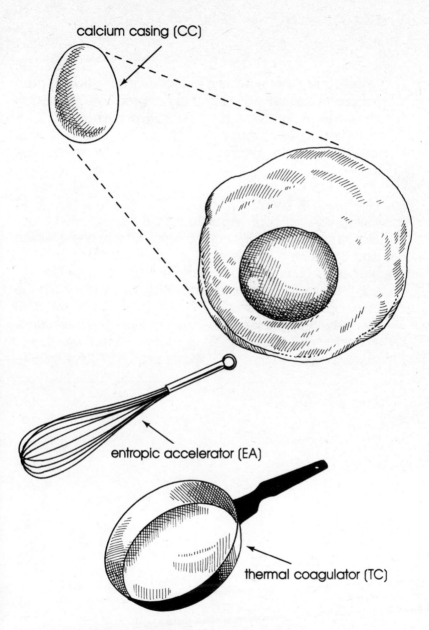

calcium casing (CC)

entropic accelerator (EA)

thermal coagulator (TC)

Avian Embryo Nutrient Cartridge

23

The (amorphous-) **fused-silicate gravitational containment vessel** (FSGCV) is a nongraduated, vitreous-state thermally depressed hydrative cylindrical fluid-ingestion system, activated by partial brachial/ulnar rotation or by the optional vacuum-induction oral delivery tube.

Tech-Speak Note

Nongravitational reactively and nonreactively operated closed metallic containment vessels, one of which cost $14 million to develop, delivered carbon-dioxide-propelled, ambient-temperature, fructose-supplemented, theobromine-rich proprietary-formula solutions to the crew of the space shuttle *Challenger* in 1985. One consumer-beverage executive called his version "a precursor of containers to come that will use an alternate means of dispensing drinks on earth" (*Washington Post*, July 12, 1985).

uncalibrated
compressed-cellulose
pipette (UCCP) →

phase-transition
heat sinks (PTHS)

integral stabilization
layer (ISL)

Fused Silicate Gravitational Containment Vessel

The **sucrose/alkaloid stimulant kit** (SASK) is an assemblage of processed performance-enhancing noncontrolled substances producing a combination of cardiac rate augmentation, cerebral synaptic transmission acceleration, and rapid energetic activation.

The ceramic gravitational containment vessel (CGCV) serves both the short-term thermal stabilization of the psychoactive high-temperature botanical filtrate and the molecular diffusion of its reinforcement-heightening aromatics.

Dissolved sucrose in the CGCV fluid is supplemented by that enhancing the superheated-lipid-processed toroidal carbohydrate module (TCM).

Tech-Speak Note

A tannin-rich solution may be produced in the CGCV with a "porous container of a dry infusion commodity," as it is called in U.S. Patents 2,728,670 and 2,728,671.

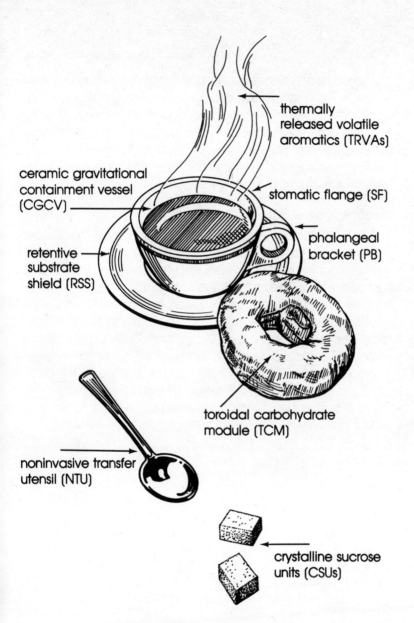

thermally released volatile aromatics (TRVAs)

ceramic gravitational containment vessel (CGCV)

stomatic flange (SF)

phalangeal bracket (PB)

retentive substrate shield (RSS)

toroidal carbohydrate module (TCM)

noninvasive transfer utensil (NTU)

crystalline sucrose units (CSUs)

Sucrose/Alkaloid Stimulant Kit

The **carbohydrate-laminated bovine protein wafer** (CLBPW) is a thermally processed, homogenized, lipid-rich, contractile-fiber-coagulated, acidified-vegetable-enhanced, farinaceous-buffered, constant-diameter thin-profile ruminant muscular-tissue disk for anthropoid mandibular-dental abrasive homogenization and enzymatic-acidic preabsorptive emulsification.

Tech-Speak Notes

CLBPW vendors, ignoring obvious marketing opportunities, have so far opposed implementation of legislatively mandated Tech Speak. "Labeling a menu item with a lot of technical terms that may be, and probably are, unfamiliar to the consumer creates confusion and raises the specter of fear without any reason for it," according to the chairman and president of the U.S. National Restaurant Association (*USA Today,* June 28, 1985).

Packagers of CLBPWs have been more enlightened, having persuaded the U.S. Department of Agriculture to let them replace the words "powdered bone" with "calcium" (*Quarterly Review of Doublespeak,* January 1984).

28

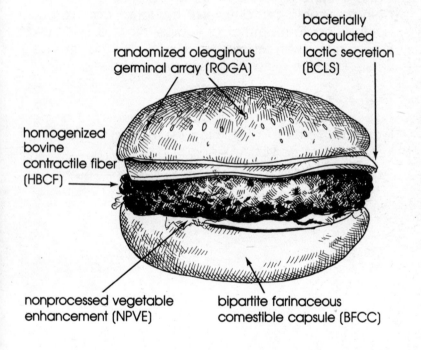

randomized oleaginous germinal array (ROGA)

bacterially coagulated lactic secretion (BCLS)

homogenized bovine contractile fiber (HBCF)

nonprocessed vegetable enhancement (NPVE)

bipartite farinaceous comestible capsule (BFCC)

Carbohydrate-Laminated Bovine Protein Wafer

Structures are ferrous, nonferrous, crystalline, and polymeric three-dimensional Euclidean-space-embedded tension/compression-sustaining, force-transmitting element assemblies.

The **canine seclusion habitat** (CSH) is a detached anthropogenic quadrilateral territorial carnivorous-companionate-mammal protective module deployed in conjunction with olfactory/sonic-activated real-time perimeter-intrusion annunciator system procedures.

Tech-Speak Note

For a proposed macro-feline "wide-range motion-detection audio-monitoring system," see S. Harris's rendering in *American Scientist,* July–August 1984, 377.

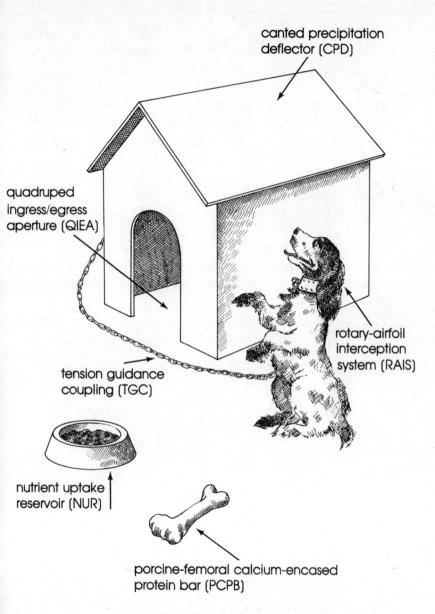

canted precipitation
deflector (CPD)

quadruped
ingress/egress
aperture (QIEA)

rotary-airfoil
interception
system (RAIS)

tension guidance
coupling (TGC)

nutrient uptake
reservoir (NUR)

porcine-femoral calcium-encased
protein bar (PCPB)

Canine Seclusion Habitat

The **passive solar illumination assembly** (PSIA) is a vertically installed, moisture-resistant photon-transmission aperture for sub-exospheric microclimate monitoring, with polished planar transparent amorphous-fused-silicate surfaces and manually adjustable gaseous infiltration/exfiltration capability.

Tech-Speak Note

In 1983 the U.S. Internal Revenue Service accused a leading accounting firm of improperly qualifying for tax credits by referring to PSIAs as "decorative fixtures," doors as "movable partitions," and shopping-center signs as "identifying devices" (*Quarterly Review* of Doublespeak, January 1984).

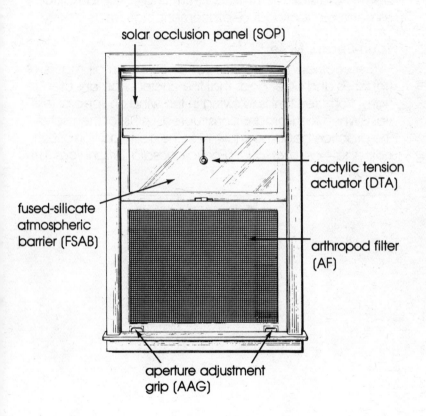

solar occlusion panel (SOP)

dactylic tension actuator (DTA)

fused-silicate atmospheric barrier (FSAB)

arthropod filter (AF)

aperture adjustment grip (AAG)

Passive Solar Illumination Assembly

The **kinesthetic anharmonic oscillator** (KAO) is a user-activated, atmospherically/frictionally damped tandem-pendular rhythmic self-limiting large-amplitude somatic bidirectional displacement platform.

Tech-Speak Note

The original *oscilla* ("little faces") were small masks of Bacchus and other gods that the ancient Romans used to hang from tree limbs to swing in the wind on special festivals. When the Romans constructed KAOs for themselves, the practice became known—in the best tradition of Latin coinage—as *oscillatio* (*Encyclopædia Britannica*, 11th edition).

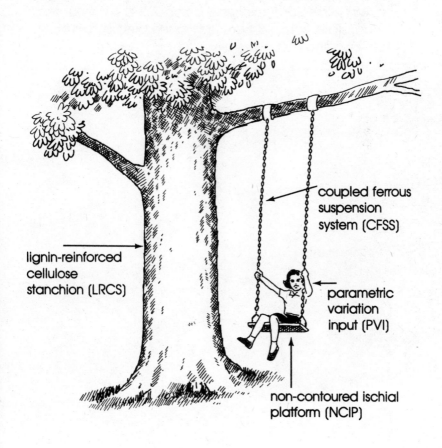

lignin-reinforced
cellulose
stanchion (LRCS)

coupled ferrous
suspension
system (CFSS)

parametric
variation
input (PVI)

non-contoured ischial
platform (NCIP)

Kinesthetic Anharmonic Oscillator

The **accreted crystalline anthropoid homologue** (ACAH) is a solar-recyclable compacted aqueous transitional-state hominid isomorph assembled as a juvenile peer-bonding mechanism.

manual particulate
concentrator (MPC)

cranial thermal gasket

carbon ocular
surrogates (COS)

apical hypocotylous
proboscoid prosthesis
(AHPP)

thoracic
segment (TS)

pedimental
formation (PF)

Accreted Crystalline Anthropoid Homologue

Protective systems (PSs) are multiple-layered, user-installable, personally configured somatic enhancements, peripherals, atmospheric and optical filters, solar radiation inhibitors, exogenous impact attenuators, sensory transduction apparatus, microclimate thermoregulatory devices, small-area precipitation-management surfaces, and mechanical interfaces, with or without semiotic display.

An important class of PSs consists of chromatically differentiated, homogenized spun cellulose, protein, and anthropogenic polymeric fibers incorporated in lapped, fiber-bonded two-dimensional reinforced matrices as conformal meta-integumental surfaces.

The **thoracic convection facilitator** (TCF) is a somesthetic continuous anisotropic hygroscopic orthogonal-mesh spun-cellulose epidermal thermoregulatory diaphoresis-management layer capable of chromatic differentiation and dorsoventral alphanumeric and other semiotic enhancement, shown here under gravitational loading after high-temperature frictionally/vibrationally accelerated anionic surfactant processing.

Tech-Speak Note

There is a publication called *Textile Maintenance Reporter,* which had 2,713 subscribers in 1985.

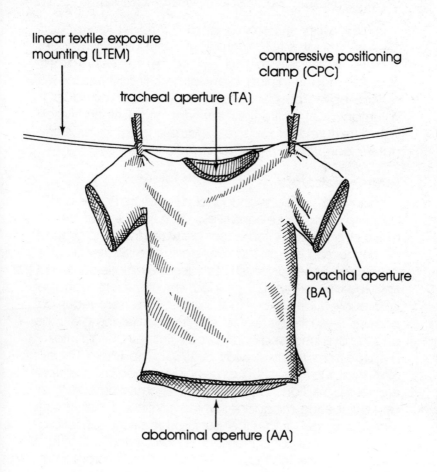

linear textile exposure
mounting (LTEM)

compressive positioning
clamp (CPC)

tracheal aperture (TA)

brachial aperture
(BA)

abdominal aperture (AA)

Thoracic Convection Facilitator

Locomotory support platforms (LSPs) are paired, nonsuperimposably isomorphic frictional somatic accelerated-gait controlled-displacement dynamic-equilibrium-maintaining bipedal terrestrial interfaces of bovine-epidermis-reinforced polyamides bonded to voluntary-contractile-tissue-driven, gravitationally activated textured propulsive-surface-engaging crosslinkable-linear-high-polymer substrates.

Tech-Speak Note

In May 1985, Adidas announced the Micro Pacer, a $125 LSP with a pressure-sensitive switch in the midsole for measuring energy interactions between foot and ground. It is connected to a microprocessor in one LSP for calculating average speed, length of stride, and calorie consumption. The company's U.S. product-development manager was quoted as saying that "runners are very technical people. They always record how many miles they've gone and the calories used compared with their dietary intake" (*Philadelphia Inquirer*, May 5, 1985). The Micro Pacer's $200 rival, the Puma RS, has been described as "a peripheral for Apple II and Commodore 64 home computers" by an engineering magazine, which continued that its software package "guides the user through a series of calibration experiments and then stores parameters . . . onto a disk." Of course the Puma RS has "a custom programmable logic array" (*IEEE Spectrum*, September 1985).

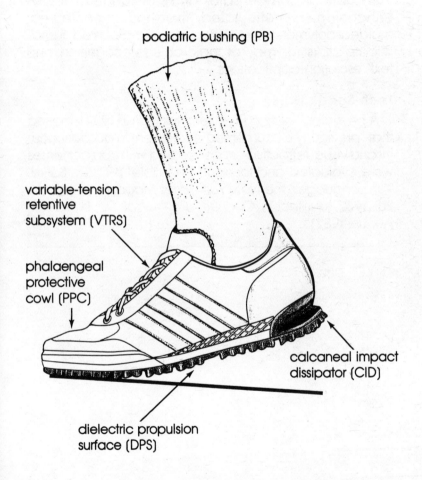

podiatric bushing (PB)

variable-tension
retentive
subsystem (VTRS)

phalaengeal
protective
cowl (PPC)

calcaneal impact
dissipator (CID)

dielectric propulsion
surface (DPS)

Locomotory Support Platforms

41

The **stereoscopic image correction system** (SICS) is a user-installable, collapsible, free-standing cranially positioned pre-corneal refractive binocular visible-spectrum optical compensator array of tandem acuity-enhancing, nonreticulated, fixed-focus, contoured, molded-polymer- or extruded-metallic-mounted fused-silicate disks for macroscopic-object-recognition and text-resolution applications.

Tech-Speak Note

A physician treating President Reagan in 1982 reported that "previously documented decrement in auditory acuity and visual refractive error corrected with contact lenses were evaluated and found to be stable" (William Safire, "On Language," the *New York Times Magazine,* February 28, 1982, quoted in *Quarterly Review of Doublespeak,* August 1982).

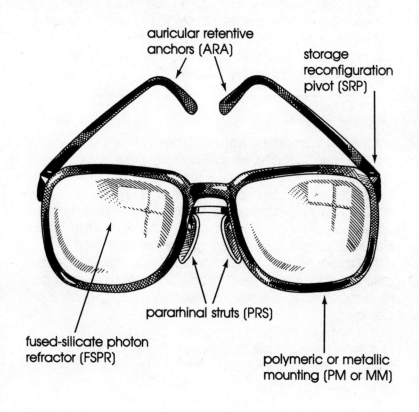

auricular retentive
anchors (ARA)

storage
reconfiguration
pivot (SRP)

pararhinal struts (PRS)

fused-silicate photon
refractor (FSPR)

polymeric or metallic
mounting (PM or MM)

Stereoscopic Image Correction System

Kinesiological transduction artifacts (KTAs) are three-dimensional friction-, convection-, and gravitation-influenced, short-range, ergonomically propelled and guided, radially symmetric, interpersonally and personally driven variable-trajectory targets.

Kinetic demonstration devices (KDDs) are macroscopic objects actively and passively deployed in real time.

The aerostatic membrane (AM) is a (synthetic-) latex, anthropogenic-carbon-dioxide- or helium-distended spherical pressure vessel with a multistranded spun-cellulose phalangeal-linked guidance coupling.

The rotary airfoil (RA) is a manually/brachially propelled, gyroscopically stabilized motor-coordination- and canine-macroscopic-object-retrieval-capability-evaluation device.

The angular momentum conservation device (AMCD) is a tandem axis-mounted, nonpropulsive, phalanx-suspended, metacarpal-controlled equiradial translation bearing.

Tech-Speak Note

See Stancil E. D. Johnson, M.D., *Frisbee: A Practitioner's Manual and Definitive Treatise* (New York: Workman Publishing Co., 1975), for the Tech-Speak nomenclature of the RA, including *cupola, flight plate,* and *flight ridges.* Dr. Johnson uses many proper names—*Lines of Headrick, Mound of Malafronte*—a peculiarity of medical Tech Speak.

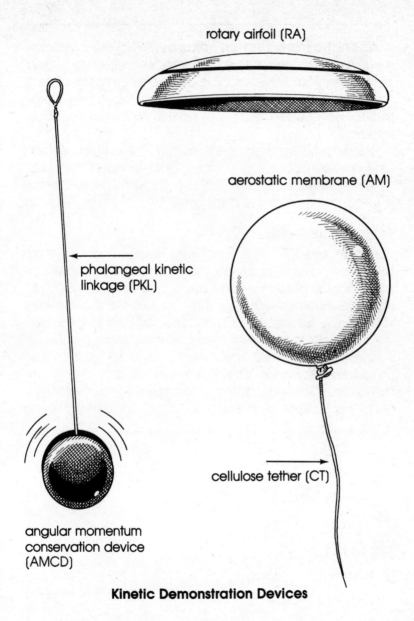

rotary airfoil (RA)

aerostatic membrane (AM)

phalangeal kinetic
linkage (PKL)

cellulose tether (CT)

angular momentum
conservation device
(AMCD)

Kinetic Demonstration Devices

45

Agonistic transduction nexuses (ATNs) are standardized, socially interactive, marker-calibrated real-time biomechanical Newtonian velocity-change projectiles.

The equine-epidermal sphere (ES) is a unibrachially propelled, atmospherically damped Bernoulli-effect collision target.

The porcine-epidermal ellipsoid (PE) is an atmospherically pressurized, aerodynamic, gore-bonded ellipsoid.

The synthetic-latex disk (SD) is a thin-profile cylinder for low-friction hydroplane deployment.

Tech-Speak Notes

As admirers of Tom Lehrer's "Fight Fiercely, Harvard" can attest, the porcine-epidermal ellipsoid is more precisely a spheroid, as ellipsoids may have other shapes. The U.S. National Football League rule book calls it a *prolate* spheroid. A sphere, in fact, is a special kind of ellipsoid.

According to the *Wall Street Journal,* manager Dave Johnson of the New York Mets prefers to call an ES-propulsion professional's hot streak a "favorable-chance deviation" ("Technology in the Workplace: A Special Report," September 16, 1985).

---

porcine epidermal
spheroid (PES)

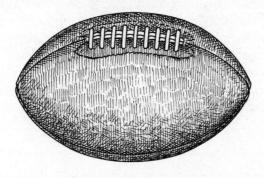

Bernoulli-effect
tesselated joint (BETJ)

equine epidermal
sphere (EES)

semi-rigid polymeric
disk (SRPD)

Agonistic Transduction Nexuses

Tools are manually activated, analogue tactile/optical feedback-controlled, cerebrospinally coordinated, contractile-tissue-powered voluntary-device-fabrication, materials-manipulation, environmental modification, exploratory-disassembly, substance-ablation, and friction-limitation technologies.

Instruments are self-regulated, real-time quantification, telemetering, and empirical parameter-determination calibrated-readout gauges.

The **dynamic load impact device** (DLID) is a centripetally effected rapid-deceleration iterative inelastic-collision generator for short-range ferrous cylinder bonding.

The torque applicator (TA) is an inelastic polymer-anchored ferrous rotational-input/translational-output circular-section axial thrust transmitter.

The keratin ablation plane (KAP) is a polished ferrous bilaterally symmetric maxillo-mandibular integumental protein-fiber sectioning tool for follicular excrescence truncation.

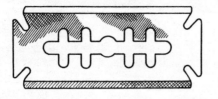

keratin ablation plane (KAP)

Prehensile-Adapted Force Transmission Devices I

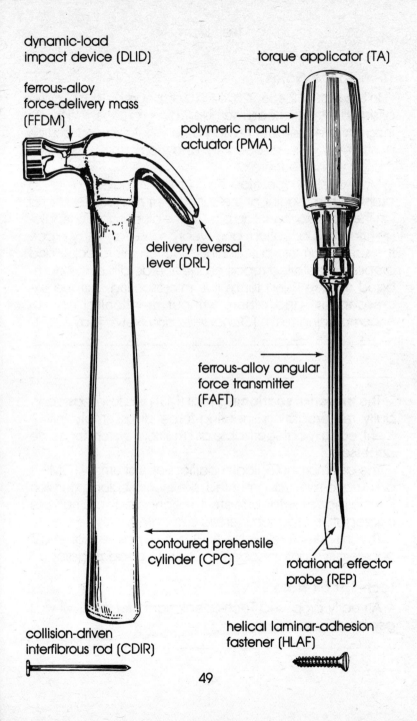

dynamic-load
impact device (DLID)

ferrous-alloy
force-delivery mass
(FFDM)

torque applicator (TA)

polymeric manual
actuator (PMA)

delivery reversal
lever (DRL)

ferrous-alloy angular
force transmitter
(FAFT)

contoured prehensile
cylinder (CPC)

rotational effector
probe (REP)

collision-driven
interfibrous rod (CDIR)

helical laminar-adhesion
fastener (HLAF)

49

Tech-Speak Notes

In U.S. Patent 2,656,225, a DLID appears as "a tool comprising a metallic head member having an opening therein, a handle member having a non-metallic end portion positioned in said opening and conforming approximately in shape thereto. . . ."

"A machine operator, having just removed a failed bushing, may squint at the surface, mutter 'scuffed,' and loft the part into the scrap bin. On the other hand, a tribology [friction, lubrication, and wear] consultant may place the same part into a scanning electron microscope and prepare a detailed report on the fine details of the damaged surface using terms like microscoring, surface excrescences, and others without mentioning an all-encompassing term" (*Standardization News*, May 1985).

The **material sectioning tool** (MST) is a low-mass, carpally reciprocating shearing-force disassembly instrument, equally categorizable as a nutrient-system ingestive accessory.

The geomorphological modification instrument (GMI) is a somatic-mass-augmented skeletomuscular extension for palmar/plantar-effected mechanical multiphase aggregative organomineralic substrate exposure.

The infrastructure probe (ISP) is an invasive high-mass accelerative anthropogenic-substrate disaggregator.

Tech-Speak Note

An early proposed Tech-Speak name for the GMI was *geotome.*

---

material sectioning
tool (MST)

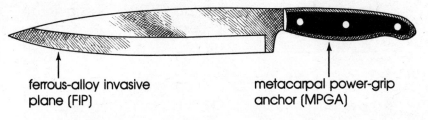

ferrous-alloy invasive
plane (FIP)

metacarpal power-grip
anchor (MPGA)

geomorphological
modification instrument (GMI)

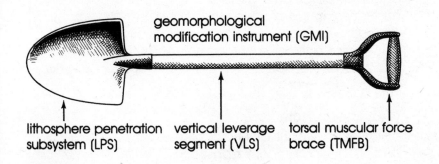

lithosphere penetration
subsystem (LPS)

vertical leverage
segment (VLS)

torsal muscular force
brace (TMFB)

infrastructure probe (IP)

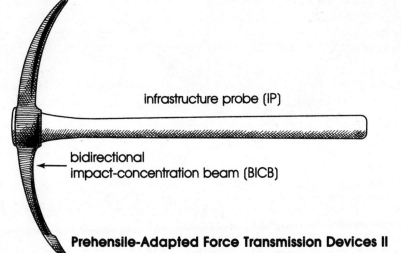

bidirectional
impact-concentration beam (BICB)

Prehensile-Adapted Force Transmission Devices II

Terrestrial rotation emulators (TREs) are apparent-solar-motion registration technologies.

The **acoustomechanical circadian regulator** (ACR) is a stored ergonomic torque-driven programmable exogenous percussive-generated fixed-pitch harmonic auditory-stimulus-production mechanism for receptor-mediated anthropoid wakefulness induction.

The solar analogue chronometer (SAC) is a duodecimally calibrated projective diurnal rotational planetary position indicator.

Tech-Speak Note

Functionally equivalent digital-readout devices should be called microprocessor-based SAC (or ACR) emulators (MACREs or MSACEs).

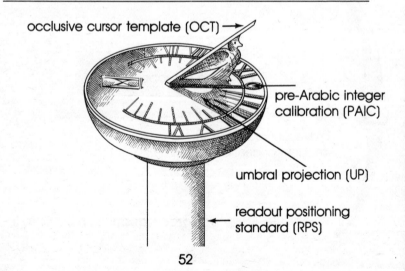

occlusive cursor template (OCT) →

pre-Arabic integer calibration (PAIC)

umbral projection (UP)

readout positioning standard (RPS)

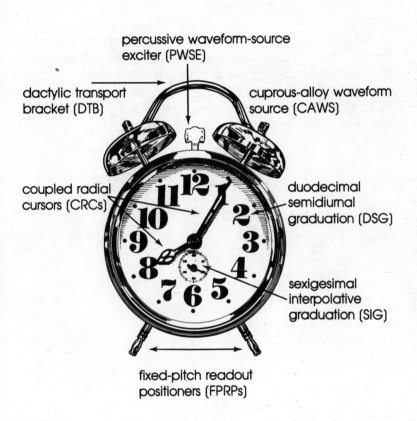

percussive waveform-source exciter (PWSE)

dactylic transport bracket (DTB)

cuprous-alloy waveform source (CAWS)

coupled radial cursors (CRCs)

duodecimal semidiurnal graduation (DSG)

sexigesimal interpolative graduation (SIG)

fixed-pitch readout positioners (FPRPs)

Terrestrial Rotation Emulators

The **equiradial translation bearing** (ETB) is a fixed-diameter friction-management device for surface atomic-adhesion reduction in macroscopic object displacement and, in force-transmission mode, for acceleration.

The two Tech-Speak hypotheses regarding the origin of the ETB are (1) polygonal approximation (PA), according to which our ancestors progressively refined initially triangular or square forms; and (2) cylindrical truncation (CT), according to which they had the right profile but needed experience in economic materials use.

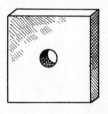

(1) polygonal approximation (PA)

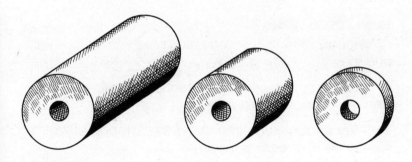

(2) cylindrical truncation (CT)

Equiradial Translation Bearing

Symbols are two-dimensional chromatic and achromatic contextually embedded, socioculturally loaded referential logograms, ideograms, pictograms, glyphs, ciphers, transcendentally encoded characters, affect releasers, microeconomic transaction tracers, and sematic vehicular flow regulators.

The **hedonic affect icon** (HAI) is a closed two-dimensional eidetic schematic pictographic noncognitive anthropoid psychosomatic-tone representation glyph, connoting self-actualized, subjectively optimal proximate-diurnal-segment expectation.

Tech-Speak Notes

A friendly Tech-Speak communicative interaction might end thus:

X: "Listener's terrestrial-rotation-interval positive emotive state maintenance proposed."

Y: "Reciprocal real-time-designated mood-elevation subroutine in operative mode."

"Face mnemonics" let researchers depict up to nineteen variables simultaneously (as nasal, ocular, oral, eyebrow, and other shape variations) in expressively variable displays. See W. H. Huggins and Doris R. Entwisle, *Iconic Communication: An Annotated Bibliography,* (Baltimore and London: The Johns Hopkins University Press, 1974, 40–42).

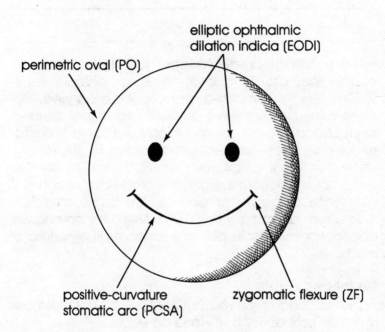

perimetric oval (PO)

elliptic ophthalmic
dilation indicia (EODI)

positive-curvature
stomatic arc (PCSA)

zygomatic flexure (ZF)

Hedonic Affect Icon

Entitlement instruments (EI) are socioeconomically conditioned, culturally authenticated value-exchange equivalency maintenance warrants.

The **universal credit voucher** (UCV) is a bilaterally pigmented, visually discriminable, graphically semi-secure, serially numbered, semiotically enhanced, discrete-valued compressed-cellulose negotiable resource microallocation instrument for non-electronic instantaneous-clearance confidential transaction facilitation.

The fractional credit voucher (FCV) is a tactile-discriminable nonferrous metallic thin-profile cylindrical UCV surrogate capable of pollical-imparted angular-momentum-driven Newtonian two-state decision-analysis applications when in bistable random-digit-generator mode.

Tech-Speak Note

The fractional credit voucher is not truly bistable, as there is a finite probability it will land on edge.

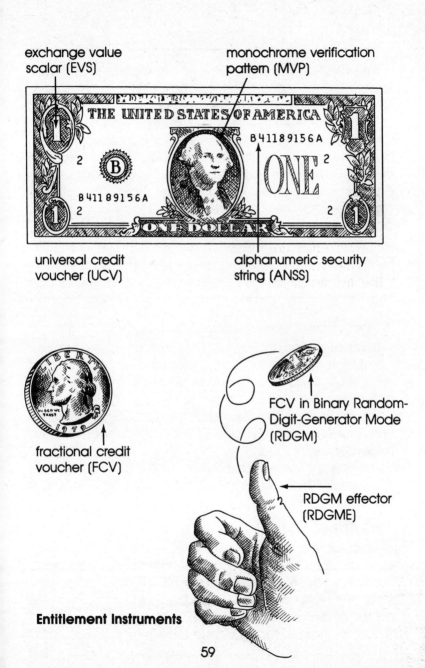

exchange value
scalar (EVS)

monochrome verification
pattern (MVP)

universal credit
voucher (UCV)

alphanumeric security
string (ANSS)

fractional credit
voucher (FCV)

FCV in Binary Random-
Digit-Generator Mode
(RDGM)

RDGM effector
(RDGME)

Entitlement Instruments

59

Information throughputs (ITs) are alphanumeric message transfer facilitators, hard-copy generation and storage technologies, intersubjective communication buffers, affect denotation displays, bionic expert system emulators, neuromuscular data-presentation servomechanisms, natural-language hermeneutic modules, voice message encoder/decoders, connotative semiotic lexicons, kinesic illustrator proxies, real-time input-output matrices, analogue information streams, interactive channels, asynchronous oral-aural links, general-purpose transmission environments, data acquisition and entry procedures, phonemic registration apparatus, together with related media and ergonomic peripherals.

Inscriptive technologies (ITs) are dactylically manipulated high-contrast substance reservoirs for semiotic and representational modification of planar compressed-cellulose substrates.

The compressed-graphite field plotter (CGFP) is a lignin/cellulose-encased crystalline carbon allotrope for shear force deposition.

The linear pigment-deposition tube (LPDT) is a microspherically transferred viscous-substance-dispersion penetrative system.

Tech-Speak Note

An alternate Texpression for the CGFP was proposed as early as March 1972 in the journal *Instruments and Control Systems: plotter/encoder/notator* for *ciphers, icons,* and *letters* (PENCIL), which was to be used with a *passive accumulative permanent/erasable raster* (PAPER). (Cited in the *Journal of Irreproducible Results,* 28:3 [1983], 31.)

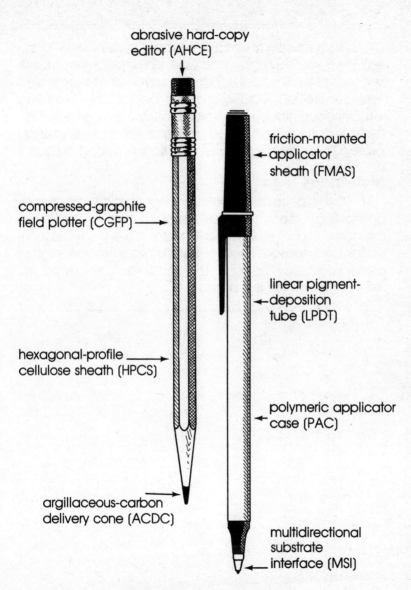

abrasive hard-copy
editor (AHCE)

friction-mounted
applicator
sheath (FMAS)

compressed-graphite
field plotter (CGFP)

linear pigment-
deposition
tube (LPDT)

hexagonal-profile
cellulose sheath (HPCS)

polymeric applicator
case (PAC)

argillaceous-carbon
delivery cone (ACDC)

multidirectional
substrate
interface (MSI)

Inscriptive Technologies

The **hard-copy multitask window array** (HMWA) is a sedentary-mode ergonomic work station for interruptable sequential bio-optical scanning, psychomotor-actuated text generation, and arithmetic operations, featuring visually discriminable nonvolatile off-line storage with prehensile data retrieval, and operator-resident processing protocols for alphanumeric/graphic inputs and outputs.

Tech-Speak Note

The Cyborg, trade name of an ergonomic somatic task positioning system, features "weight-activated hydraulic cylinders," an "electronic control core . . . factory-calibrated sensors, and a light-emitting-diode digital position display option." The manufacturer, Rudd International, still calls it a chair.

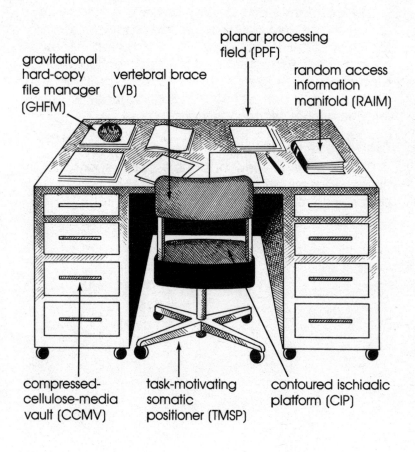

gravitational
hard-copy
file manager
(GHFM)

vertebral brace
(VB)

planar processing
field (PPF)

random access
information
manifold (RAIM)

compressed-
cellulose-media
vault (CCMV)

task-motivating
somatic
positioner (TMSP)

contoured ischiadic
platform (CIP)

Hard-Copy Multitask Window Array

The **calcium** (-carbonate) **trace display system** (CTDS) is a neuromuscular-driven text/graphics generator for deposition of fossilized biominerals on a planar metamorphic substrate for orally/aurally/optically-mediated transmission to multiple compressed-graphite field plotters and linear pigment deposition tubes in an intergenerational information induction cell.

Tech-Speak Note

The *Quarterly Review of Doublespeak* reports that in current educational usage this process may be followed by "criterion reference testing" (October 1984).

vertical inscriptive
surface (VIS)

calcium trace display
cursor (CTDC)

$$y = 4\lambda x(1-x)$$

semiotic recycling
block (SRB)

compressed-calcium
cylinder (CCC)

calcium trace display
professional (CTDP)

Calcium Trace Display System

USING TECH SPEAK

When Tech Speak was still young, Alfred Lord Tennyson wrote:

> Flower in the crannied wall,
> I pluck you out of the crannies,
> I hold you here, root and all, in my hand,
> Little flower—but *if* I could understand
> What you are, root and all, and all in all,
> I should know what God and man is.

Fortunately for poetry, Tennyson did not know that in Tech Speak the flower is readily understandable: it is among other things a (probably negatively geotropic) lithophyte.

Tech Speak is still of little use in verse, but it does marvels for prose. Words don't stagger forth as choppy Anglo-Saxon syllables; they positively roll. Sprinkling your writing and conversation with Tech Speak makes every phrase count. And it isn't hard to do.

How to Speak Tech

Putting together Tech-Speak words—concatenating Texpressions, to give the process its proper name—isn't as hard as it looks, just as in Vernacular English, a small number of roots, prefixes, and suffixes can be recombined to describe a vast number of people, things, and situations. Also, as in Vernacular English, users may choose among several alternative forms and may disagree about which is most appropriate or elegant.

A Texpression should name something as though you, the speaker, had just invented it. It should give as accurate an idea as possible of the structure and function of what you are talking about.

If you look back at the Tech-Speak definitions in the first part of this book, you will notice that some are imprecise. The core of a *carbohydrate-laminated bovine protein wafer* (CBPW) might have more lipids than proteins. The physics of the *kinesthetic anharmonic oscillator* (KAO) are barely described in its name; in fact they were difficult enough to merit a paper in a respected physics journal and a report in *Scientific American.* Is a spinning *fractional credit voucher* (FCV) really random when its outcome is heads or tails—I mean, capital or caudal? Some statisticians think it's not chance at all; skilled magicians can control which way the FCV lands.

Tech Speak, in other words, is linguistic engineering, and engineering (unlike science) is informed compromise. Few if any Texpressions will be exactly right. Compromise also governs the length of Texpressions. They should not be too long to remember, and they should roll off the tongue; in other words, they are mnemonically and prosodically constrained. Between five and fifteen syllables is usually right. If you have more ideas than that, save them for either a separate definition, an alternate Texpression for the same thing, or a Texpression for a related thing.

A Tech-Speak Generative Algorithm: The Semantic Crystal Module

Theoretical linguistics—a discipline that has contributed immensely to Tech Speak already—gives us a model for assembling Texpressions. Dr. Janice Moulton and Dr. George M. Robinson have developed Syntax Crystal Modules as part of their model of language organization. Moulton and Robinson's modules are sets of rules, each with its own word list, for stringing together new phrases from different social or literary situations. They are like computer programs and could in fact be computerized. The Deli Module, for instance, yields phrases like HOT COFFEE AND A BLT WITH COLE SLAW ON RYE and A DOUBLE ORDER ON RYE AND COLE SLAW. (See their *Organization of Language*.)

There are also Porno and Philosophy modules, among others. Applied to Tech Speak, the Syntax Crystal concept generates Texpressions rather than stringing them together in sentences that follow the rules of Vernacular English.

Seeding the Crystal

To start a Texpression, begin with the last word rather than the first. This is the crystal seed, also called a *substantor*. (In Vernacular English it is called a noun.) For example, *platform* is the seed of *locomotory support platforms* (LSPs) above. We could have started with any of several other seeds—*interface, device, assembly, subsystem*—but *platforms* seemed worth trying first. It's specific, it's far from any Vernacular English synonym for these macroscopic objects, it's unlikely to be overused for other

69

Texpressions, and (as a static word for something that's supposed to be dynamic) it's unexpected, or, in Tech Speak, counterintuitive.

Nobody can be sure a substantor is a good Tech-Speak seed until modifiers—adjectives, nouns used as adjectives, and adverbs—are attached, because the aptness of a Texpression depends even more on the modifiers than on the substantor. If you're disappointed with the modifiers that can be applied to a substantor, start over with another. Since Tech Speak readily turns nouns into adjectives, a discarded substantor can always be reintroduced as a modifier.

Let's say you want a Texpression for *bowling ball*. You might try *sphere* first, adding *brachially propelled* and *digitally released,* and perhaps *high-mass.* But the resulting phrase has disadvantages. It might apply, for instance, to a baseball or even the hammer-throw. In fact, there are too many spheres around. The best Texpressions are unique.

So let's start again, this time with a seed referring to the macroscopic object's effect, not to its form. We try *destabilizer.* Are the right modifiers available? If we describe the things it strikes as *pylons,* definitely! The object turns out to be an *intertial sequential pylon destabilizer* and its target an *arithmetically progressive semi-stable pylon array.*

A Tech-Speak seed may also depend on its context. For instance, a self-anchored photosynthetic structure is a *lignin-reinforced cellulose stanchion* when it supports a *kinesthetic damped anharmonic oscillator.* In another situation, though, we might have called it a *pressurized-fluid microclimate stabilizer.*

Crystal Rules

Once you have a trial Tech-Speak substantor, there are at least three types of modifiers that can accompany it:

1. Another substantor as its pair. Many or most Texpressions start this way: *rotor* assembly, *guidance* coupling, *window* array. In the predecessor of Tech Speak called Space Speak, three, four, or more substantors may be nested in this way.

2. Structors suggest how it is organized or what it is made of: *cellulose* rotor assembly, *flexible* guidance coupling, *hard-copy* window array.

3. Processors describe how it works: *atmospheric* cellulose rotor assembly, *tensile* guidance coupling, hard-copy *multitask* window array.

4. Qualifiers say more about the process. To any of the above Texpressions we could add *enhanced* or *advanced*—or, if they aren't, *conventional.*
You don't need each of these for every Texpression, but you should consider for variety at least a few of each. They may be either nouns or adjectives.
In *carbohydrate-laminated bovine protein wafer* (CBPW), the first two modifiers (*carbohydrate* and *laminated*) and the second two (*bovine* and *protein*) are both structors. In *calcium trace display, trace* is a processor and *calcium* a structor modifying it. Which elements you choose depends on the substantor with which you begin.

TECH SPEAK

As a flow chart, a Tech Speak crystal would look like this:

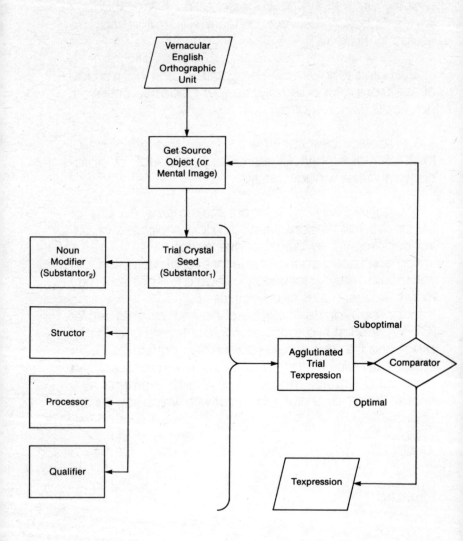

Tech-Speak Crystal Seeds

Tech-Speak crystal seeds are all substantors, and any noun not used in a Vernacular English sense can be a crystal seed. Some of these are especially versatile higher-order words that can always be used if nothing else comes to mind. In fact, this is their only problem. They are so vague, and thus so generally applicable, that Tech Speakers risk overapplying them. It's a good idea not to try them until and unless you've exhausted the alternatives. We can call them the *default roots:*

unit	cell	module	station
system	subsystem	device	structure
facilitator	effector	actuator	agent
substance	framework	matrix	node
vector	medium	transducer	instrument
mechanism	input	output	throughput
habitat	environment	assembly	commodity
artifact	nexus	icon	tool
aggregation	event	component	technology
configuration	parameter	increment	decrement

Active Substantors

Before trying a default root, consider more specific words as Tech-Speak seeds. The following may be suitable for macroscopic objects that do things to other MOs:

exchanger	generator	modulator	initiator
manipulator	converter	circulator	annunciator
stabilizer	separator	homogenizer	compactor
abrader	ablator	deflector	detonator
probe	positioner	coagulator	plane
multiplexer	releaser	radiator	exciter
irradiator	restraint	incubator	centrifuge
controller	cavitator	rectifier	vibrator
sectioner	dilator	fractionator	suppressor
evaporator	oxidizer	atomizer	reducer
agitator	emitter	condenser	integrator
donor	accelerator	tractor	retractor
propeller	impeller	depressant	extruder

Transmission Substantors

Transmission substantors are semi-active:

transponder	conductor	buffer	interface
bearing	reflector	nozzle	grating
simulator	emulator	emplacement	locator
distributor	protector	orbiter	filter
motivator	attenuator	supply	plotter
brace	cursor	source	template

Passive Substantors

Passive substantors are acted on, or are the scene of action:

substrate	wafer	barrier	projectile
arc	flexure	grating	cylinder
residue	tunnel	ring	sensor
gauge	surface	baffle	conductor
scalar	block	sheath	pipette
bracket	flange	beam	pattern
cone	layer	vessel	aromatic (n.)
segment	graduation	projection	calibration
standard	readout	indicia	voucher
turret	prism	quadrant	truss
column	compound	tank	reservoir
mast	bar	yoke	membrane
chamber	medium	cartridge	armature
framework	grid	network	lattice
strut	hood	canopy	manifold
anchor	base	vessel	accumulator
facility	detector	set	subset
aggregate	array	database	compound
complex	shield	support	medium
voucher	tube	panel	joint
recipient	port	sink	particle
pylon	vault	stanchion	target

Vocationals

Of course, people are substantors, too, but in their occupations and not as human beings. A person who isn't a juvenile or an emeritus(-ta) is a:

professional	technician	analyst
operator	representative	officer
practitioner	consultant	associate

Structors

After you have a trial substantor or two, it's time to look for structors. Because most Tech-Speak substantors are bland, it's the structors that give a Texpression its character.

Like Tech-Speak roots, some structural modifiers risk being overused but are still indispensable.

Origin	anthropogenic
	nonanthropogenic
	biogenic
	inorganic
State	solid-
	liquid-
	gaseous-
	mixed-
Causation	random
	stochastic
	pseudo-random
	deterministic
	endogenous
	exogenous
Form	crystalline
	amorphous (e.g., glass)
Color	monochromatic
	polychromatic
Composition	homogeneous
	heterogeneous

Miscellaneous   equilibrium
nonequilibrium
static
dynamic

To avoid monotony and include social arrangements and organized data as well as physical objects within Tech Speak, we need a range of other structors.

Tech Taxa

Linnaean classification might seem a natural source for Tech-Speak modifiers, but in fact it's not directly useful. It was intended for considering relations among species and not for adaptation as adjectives or anything else. When something is derived from or used by an animal, we must go back to the original Latin and Greek generic names for our modifiers. These are Tech Taxa.

Some Tech Taxa are easy and even commonplace:

If it relates to . . .	Then it's . . .
a cow or bull	bovine
a pig	porcine
a dog	canine
a cat	feline
a horse	equine
a lion, tiger, etc.	macro-feline
a rat, squirrel, etc.	rodent(ine)
an insect, spider, or crustacean	arthropod
a bee	apian
a spider	arachnid
an ant	formic
a fish	ichthyic
a bird	avian

If it relates to . . .	*Then it's . . .*
a chicken or turkey	gallinaceous
a pigeon	columbine
a songbird	passerine
any flowering plant	angiosperm (includes hard-wood trees)
an evergreen tree	conifer (or better still, gymnosperm, though they aren't the only ones)
grass	gramineous

Organic Materials Structors

Sometimes it's better to describe the structure of a macroscopic object in terms of its chemistry rather than of its animal or vegetable origins. Here there is more opportunity for originality, but also more potential for error.

If it's . . .	*Call it . . .*
wood	lignin-reinforced cellulose
paper	compressed- or calendered-cellulose
fatty (noticeably)	lipid
bread, etc.	carbohydrate
meat (red)	protein or contractile-tissue
sauce	colloidal
shellfish	crustacean or molluscan
eggs	avian-embryonic
peas or beans	leguminous
carrots	umbelliferous
potatoes	tuberous
peaches or cherries	drupaceous
pecans, walnuts, or macadamia nuts	cotyledonal
mushrooms	fungal

milk	lactose-solution
salt	saline
pepper	capsicum
white or brown sugar	sucrose
sugar in soft drinks	fructose or sucrose
sugar in other foods	glucose or sucrose

tobacco, chocolate, psy-
   choactive drugs
	alkaloid (or caffeine, nico-
	   tine, etc.)

an alcoholic drink	ethanol

Here especially, Tech-Speak style requires sacrificing strict scientific accuracy. Most foods and other organic materials have lots of other chemicals in them. In fact, reading packaged-food ingredients labels is excellent Tech-Speak preparation, even if you can't use actual lists that long.

Other Materials

Most macroscopic objects have a gross structure easy to name in Tech Speak. If you can't or don't want to be more specific, here are some good alternatives:

If it's . . .	Call it . . .
stainless steel	ferrous-chromium-alloy
cast iron	ferrous-carbon-alloy
plastic	polymer
nylon	polyamide
polyester	synthetic-resin
porcelain	ceramic
glass	fused-silicate or vitreous
paper	compressed- or laminar- cellulose
rubber	crosslinkable-high-polymer
stretch	elastomer

If it's . . .	*Call it* . . .
cotton	spun-cellulose
wool	ovine-keratin-protein
leather	acid-preserved bovine (etc.)-epidermal
glue	bonding-adhesive

Processors

Because macroscopic objects have a way of doing things to each other, many Texpressions aren't complete without one or more processors that begin to explain what's happening or the source of action. Here's a short list of things that can happen:

If something . . .	*Call it* . . .
hits something that stops it	rapid deceleration
propels something else from rest	acceleration
twists something	torsion
makes something slide in two	shear
presses on something	compression
stretches something	tension

These Newtonian processors can be some of Tech Speak's trickiest units, because physicists and engineers use common words like force, energy, power, stress, strain, mass, and weight rigorously, and most of the time the rest of us don't. Stress and strain are not identical, for example; the first is what produces the second. Inertia is any motion of an object with constant velocity, e.g., standing still. A force is what accelerates or decelerates that object. Momentum isn't really gained or lost. Power isn't a form of energy; it's the rate at which energy is transferred. Weight is a measure of gravitational force, while mass is a measure of inertia.

If something works by . . .	Call it . . .
human force	kinesthetic
heating	thermal
cutting	ablative
burning	oxidation or combustion
freezing or even cooling	cryogenic
a falling mass	gravitational
melting, vaporizing, or con- densing	phase-transition
a combination of forces	synergetic

Somatics

Somatics are processors that refer to the human body. If a body meet a body coming through the rye—that's a somatic cereal interface. Somatics sometimes refer to the part of the body that is covered or otherwise affected by a macroscopic object, like the cranial thermal gasket and the podiatric bushing.

More often, a somatic identifies the part of the body that directs or activates some macroscopic object. Most of the time, those are the hands (manual), feet (pedal), arms (brachial), or legs (crural). As usual, Tech Speak sacrifices strict accuracy to avoid monotony by using more specific somatics, generally bones.

Why not muscles? Occasionally we can introduce them to Tech Speak—the zygomaticus, for example, which shapes the oral curve of the hedonic affect icon. But many other important muscles have compound names that would be hard to integrate into Texpressions. And muscles act together so much that it's often impossible to single one or another out. So bones it is.

If this acts . . .	Call it . . .
finger	dactylic, phalangeal, or digital

TECH SPEAK

If this acts . . .	Call it . . .
palm	metacarpal
wrist	carpal
forearm	antebrachial or ulnar
sole of foot	plantar
head	cranial
neck	cervical
lower jaw	mandibular
upper jaw	maxillary
pelvic bones (for sitting)	ischiadic
ear	otic or auricular
nose	rhinal or nasal
mouth	stomatic or oral
tongue	glossal or lingual
intestines	visceral
skin	integumental or epidermal
hair	keratin, or follicular protein
sensory organ	organoleptic

Because even Vernacular English uses some Latin forms like *oral* and *nasal*—how many critics of Tech Speak say *toothy* rather than *dental?*—and because *digital* has other meanings, Greek forms are nearly always preferable as somatics. That's why they're not called *corporeals.*

Somatics include not only body parts, but processes.

If you . . .	Call it . . .
sweat	diaphoretic
walk	locomotory
chew	masticatory
swallow	ingestive
talk	(natural-language-) communicative

Qualifiers

Tech Speak has its own qualifiers for describing processes.

If you mean . . .	Say . . .
standard, ordinary, regular	conventional
new, improved	enhanced
new and expensive	advanced
similar	isomorphic
different	allotropic
slowed	inhibited
attached	bonded or fused
protected	secure
uniform	homogeneous
helping	adjuvant
independent	autonomic
dependent	heteronomous
not continuous	discrete
shape	morphological
observed	phenomenological
audible	acoustic
really important	paradigmatic or canonical
placed	deployed
done	implemented
process limited	stabilized
equipment-related	ergonomic
in step	isochronous
on or off	binary
one after another	serial
elementary	basal
rundown	degraded
hurried	accelerated
informational	cognitive
emotional	noncognitive or cathectic

If you mean . . .	*Say . . .*
pleasurable	hedonic
body language	proxemic
communicative	semiotic
at right angles	orthogonal
divided in two	dichotomous
nondigital	analogue
gridlike	cartesian
stagnant	steady-state
solving a problem	heuristic
interpretive	hermeneutic
descriptive	synchronic
all-embracing	holistic
historical	diachronic
clock time	real-time

Prefixes

If, in composing a Texpression, you can't find the right component, try modifying another word by negating or qualifying it. The compressed-cellulose micropipette mentioned previously is, for example, *uncalibrated*. We dissolve sucrose in fluids with a *noninvasive* transfer utensil. Here are some suggestions beyond the standard negatives (*non-, un-, a-,* etc.):

If you want to say . . .	*Try . . .*
on a higher level	meta- or supra-
alongside	para-
underneath	infra- or sub-
within	intra-
big or global	macro-
small or local	micro-
foreign	exo-
internal	endo-

outside	ecto-
too much	hyper-
too little	hypo-
before	ante-
bad	dys-
good	eu-
together	syn-
different	allo- or hetero-
the same	iso- or homo-
early	proto-
middle	meso-
final	telo-

Techronyms

When you've finished concatenating a Texpression, it's usually time for a Techronym, especially if you plan to embed the idea in Vernacular English sentences. Don't worry about the sound of the Techronym, or even about whether it could be mistaken for an existing Techronym or Vernacular English Acronym (VEA). Of course it can and will be mistaken for other acronyms. Almost all combinations of two, three, and four letters that would be allowed on a license plate—and some that wouldn't. . . .

Tech Speakers have enough semantic and prosodic constraints to watch without the additional demands of acronym formation. Trying to make a clever acronym usually compromises the descriptive power of a Texpression at best, or turns cute at worst. A better technique is to omit the second part of a hyphenated phrase, as in the U.S. Army's TOW (tube-launched, optically tracked, wire-guided) missile. There is a Techronym Index at the end of this book, but Tech Speakers should feel free to modify any abbreviation suggested here if it fits their purposes. Each circle of Tech Speakers will develop its own set of Techronyms, now as always.

TEXERCISES

Now that you have seen Tech Speak in theory and practice—or rather, *praxis*—it is time to develop your agglutinative logosynthetic skills. As in learning any other language, you are best off thinking as little as possible about the words of your native (Vernacular English) language, and contemplating the macroscopic objects themselves.

Here is a series of macroscopic objects, from the small-was-beautiful technologies of our ancestors to the classics of twentieth-century design. It's time to give them and their parts some proper Tech-Speak names.

Once you have tried these, you can make Tech Speak a competitive game with friends. If you are in a macroscopic-object-rich environment, one player can point to an MO and challenge the other to give as many names as possible to it and its parts. Then the other player does the pointing. If there is no third party to keep score, each player should keep a record of his or her own Texpressions and submit them later to a referee. Or the referee can choose an MO or MO-complex and give all players, say, five minutes to note their Texpressions.

You don't even need MOs for competitive Tech Speak. You can think of occupations (butcher, baker, etc.), institutions, political movements, even religions. The more alternative Texpressions you are willing to consider, the more fun Tech Speak will be.

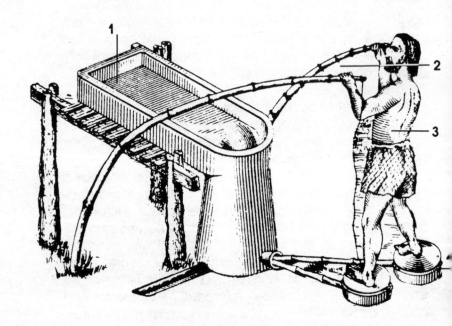

Small-Was-Beautiful Technologies

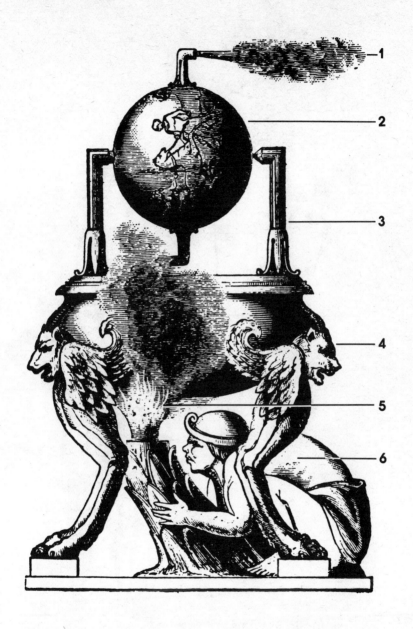

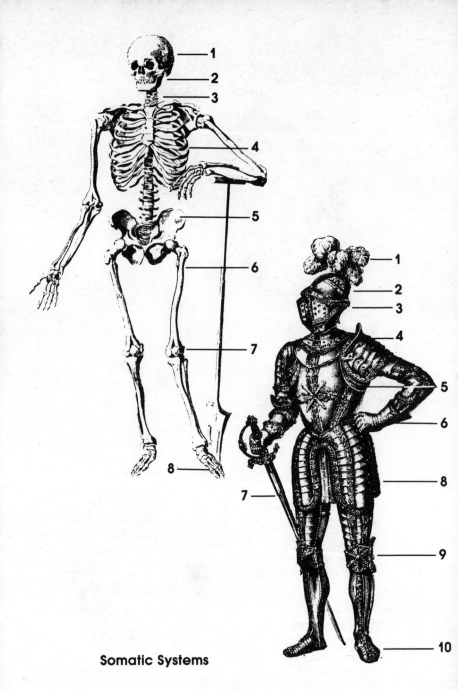

Somatic Systems

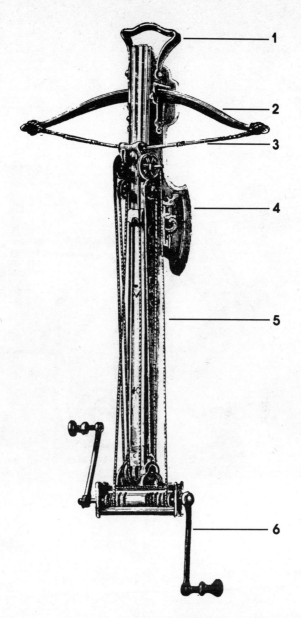

1

2

3

4

5

6

Ballistic Combat System

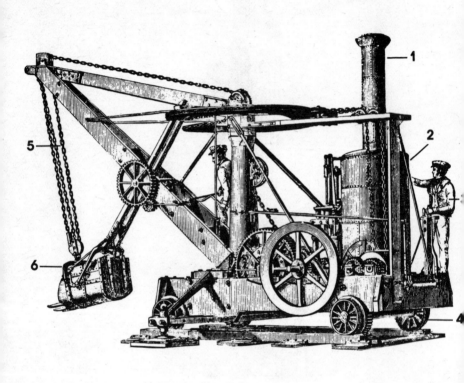

Pedosphere Manipulator

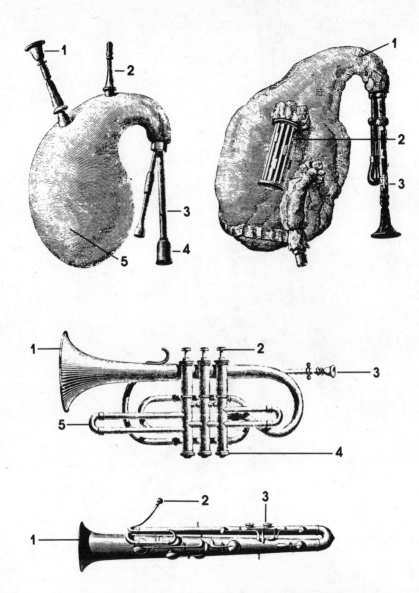

Vibrational Atmospheric Waveform Generators

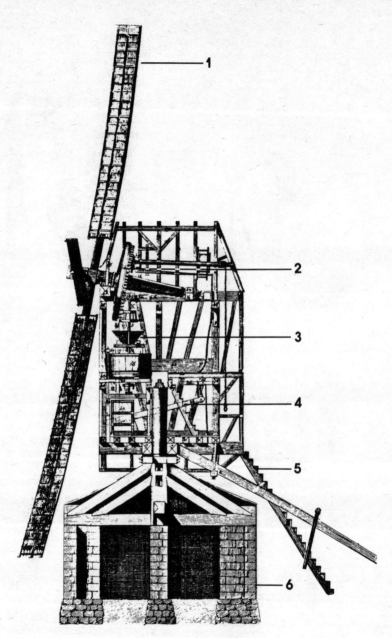

Nutrient Processors

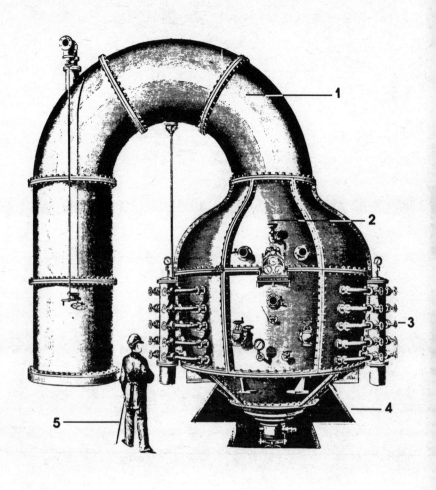

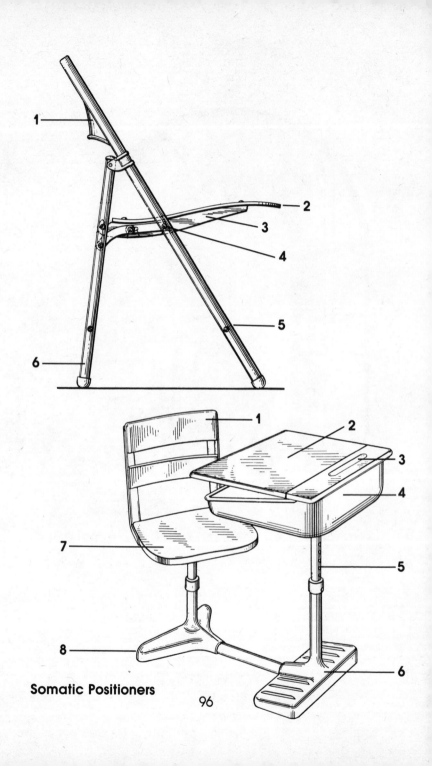

Somatic Positioners

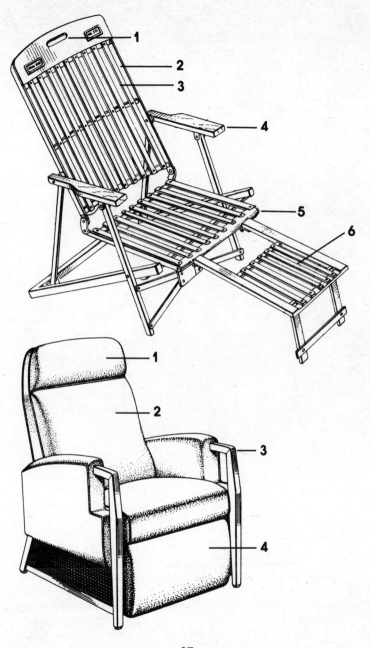

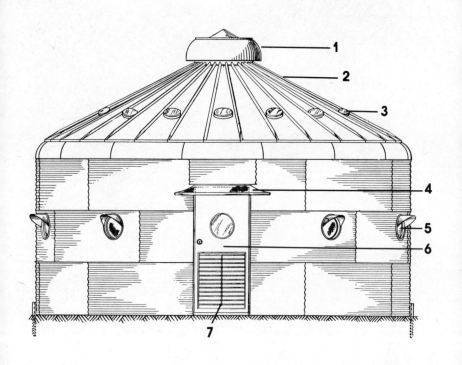

1

2

3

4

5

6

7

Dymaxial Modules

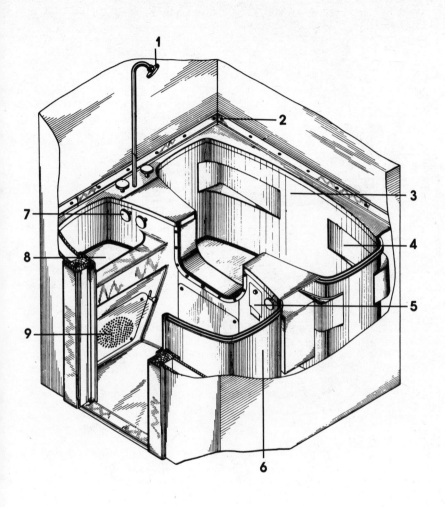

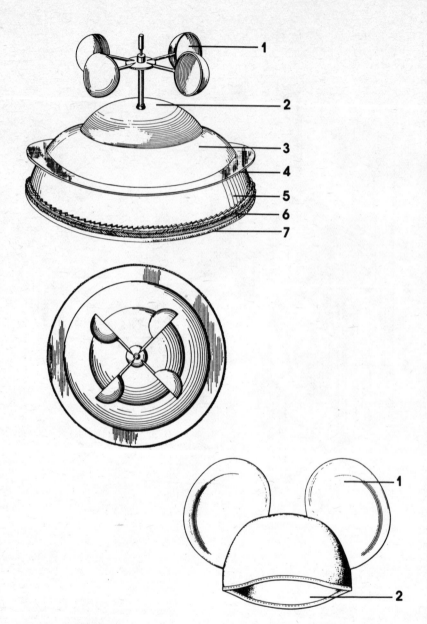

Cranial Gaskets

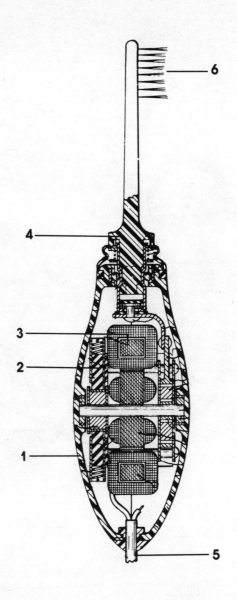

Biogenic-Enamel Maintenance Appliance

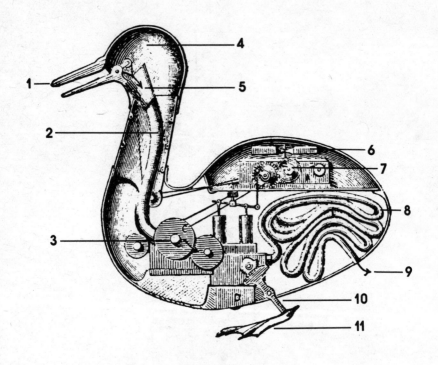

Vertebrate Emulator

NONTECHNICAL EPILOGUE

The mark of an educated English speaker is dismay at other people's usage. America's linguistic shudders move not up and down the social ladder—which is defined by possessions rather than expressions—but in a circle.

The leading critics and columnists accuse the school and college writing instructors of corrupting generations of pupils with their permissiveness, and of developing a horrid pedagoguese sociolect of their own.

The English teachers blame the decline of writing partly on the doublespeak of politicians and the gobbledygook of bureaucrats.

The more outspoken members of Congress attack scientists and engineers for introducing their jawbreaking, mystifying lexicon into military and civilian issues.

Natural scientists insist that *their* vocabulary is necessary and even economical, but has been abused by the social scientists, those false claimants to conceptual rigor.

And the social scientists, or at least the linguists among them, reject this condescension and bring usage criticism full circle by finding at least some of the language critics inconsistent, ahistoric, and snobbish.

Everybody has a place on the Usage Scorn Wheel. Almost everybody is convinced that the language has never been so degraded—by others. Our debauched vocabulary is said to contaminate every institution from the courtroom to the bedroom. It is time for the Speech Cure.

The Speech Cure

"You are what you eat," say the nutrition enthusiasts. "You are what you wear," warn the wardrobe and personal-image consultants. And usage authorities add, "You are what you say."

The Speech Cure is not new. Dennis Baron has told its story in his delightful book, *Grammar and Good Taste: Reforming the American Language.* As early as 1780, John Adams was reminding the Second Continental Congress that as government influenced language, "language in its turn influences not only the form of government, but the temper, the sentiments, and manners of the people."

Almost a century after Adams a leading language authority, Richard Grant White, was pointing out that "the mental tone of a community may be vitiated by a yielding to the use of loose, coarse, low, and frivolous phraseology." White may have been most agitated by slang, but new commercial terms also seemed a menace. He thought *petroleum* was a pretentious synonym for *rock-oil.*

Two hundred years later, neither America nor England has the language academy that Adams was promoting, and slang achieves almost instant respectability, but two other movements seem to be thriving together: a torrent of new jargon words, and a flood of newsletters, columns, and books denouncing them.

The more the language is defended, the more readily it seems to crumble. The more jeremiads are heard, the more abominations appear. The more copies of Strunk and White's *Elements of Style* are sold, the less influential it seems to be.

A television set is a *video monitor,* a monitor itself is a *cathode ray tube* (CRT). A life-saver is a *personal preservation flotation device.* A *therapeutic misadventure* (medical malpractice) ends in a *terminal episode* (death). A gangster is a member of a *career offender cartel,* at least in New Jersey. Solitary confinement is a *behavior adjustment unit.*

To language reformers, the spread of doublespeak like this is but proof of how right George Orwell was in his essay of 1946, "Politics and the English Language." Orwell acknowledged that bad thinking produces bad speech, but he added that "the slovenliness of our language makes it easier for us to have foolish thoughts."

Orwell thought that everything was political, and politics "a mass of lies, evasions, folly, hatred, and schizophrenia." He believed people could shake these habits by avoiding clichés, fancy words, and the passive voice—in other words, that they could take the Speech Cure.

While nearly all of Orwell's examples were European, his message has been taken most seriously in America. This seems odd at first, because the American love of pompous words (*elevator* rather than *lift*) has never endangered our liberties. But just as Americans went from communal drunken binges to total Prohibition in a hundred years, prolixity and purity are inseparable. Speech-reform movements are the Moral Majority of the intellectuals.

People with big vocabularies, though, overlook the benefits of jargon for the public, as the Prohibitionists begrudged the workingman his shot-and-a-beer. Giving people new phrases and metaphors to describe their feelings seems to make them feel better; the poor have a right to mid-life and identity crises, too. In fact, one psychiatrist has even claimed that psychoanalysis may be more effective with schizophrenics if it is conducted in a language (e.g., German) taught to the patient for this purpose.

Orwell considered jargon the expression of insincerity. Sometimes it is, though, as the Watergate defendants found, that evasive language backfires more often than not. The very worst jargon, Marin County psychobabble, results precisely from efforts to create an emotionally transparent, wholly honest diction. The real problem is the opposite. As some language critics acknowledge, most dictators are direct. They use simple, honest words like *home, children, blood, soil, work, iron, fate, strength, youth,* and (of course) *victory.*

Most jargonauts don't seem to be cynics, frauds, or fools. They are honest people who deeply want improvement— sometimes, to be sure, mainly self-improvement—and use their language as a platform. Skilled, well-paid workers like carpenters and plumbers haven't often sought new titles like *structural-cellulose technician* and *fluid-management engineer.* In fact, as Hugh Rawson has pointed out, merging traditional craft names in an all-purpose "technician" classification is an anti-union technique. The Teamsters are content with their ancient name and double-horse emblem. It's some window-washers (and probably not the organized, high-rise kind) who want to be called *fenestration experts.* It's the remaining elevator operators, at least at one hospital, who are called the *vertical transportation corps.*

Considering the lot of people holding a technologically

obsolete job that keeps them in moving boxes filling and emptying all day with patients, staff, and visitors, never seeing each other during work—why should they not be given some esprit de corps, a lift, as it were? Their alertness and courtesy may help run a hospital.

In politics, too, jargon is the mark of the aspiring underdog. Those securely in power have good usage on their side. Even downwardly mobile ruling classes, as the English example shows, can speak directly. Others need slogans and euphemisms: *co-determination, affirmative action, comparable worth*. When Harold Wilson eloquently invoked the "impulse cycle" of a computer and other scientific triumphs to the Labour Party Conference at Scarborough in 1963, even the conservative press noted how his language swept the delegates off their feet.

Wilson's example shows the other side of jargon, and the Speech Cure generally. Reform halts or pauses. Zeal flags. But the brave new words live to haunt their creators. Jargon reminds us too often of failed hopes. The *correctional facility* may be as dangerous and overcrowded as the old *penitentiary*, itself built to end the abuses of the former *prison*. The *building engineer* may have no more success in fixing your doorbell than his predecessor, the janitor, had. Today's speech disease is yesterday's speech cure.

Jargon as Reform:
Legalese

The law shows the paradox most clearly. When the ancient Celtic lawyers of Britain went about their mysterious rituals, their private, already archaic language was not yet jargon in our sense. It had no public life or influence. The Norman conquest, as David Mellinkoff has pointed out, brought England not (yet) technical legal French but an ambiguous, basically oral and lay language. It took two hundred years for a legal profession to emerge. At first a word in a document could mean many things. *Entendre* "could mean what we now know as intention, attention, understanding, hearing, obedience, waiting, meaning, ... purport, assumption, information, thought."

Hard as it is to believe, legalese was a reform. An emerging profession was trying to make itself clear. And it did so within its ranks, to the exclusion of everybody else. An expression like "an heir in tail rebutted from his formedon by a lineal warranty with descended assets," quoted by Mellinkoff as "the showpiece of law French precision," may have been incomprehensible, but it was not muddled.

For centuries, lay people grumbled against what a seventeenth-century writer called "hotch potch French and Latine imposed by Lawyers for their own gain to instruct few others ..., to cheat the universalitie of the Nation of their rights and understandings, and make themselves, and their Counsels most learned in others affairs."

Even in the early nineteenth century, two generations after the official abolition of law French in 1731, the philosopher Jeremy Bentham denounced lawyers' talk as "excrementitious matter" and "literary garbage," as "an instrument, an iron crow or pick-lock key, for collecting plunder in cases in which otherwise it could not be collected." Yet as Mellinkoff has observed, Bentham's drive for clearer language actually was responsible for some of today's legalese. For example, Bentham believed that "a verb slips through your fingers like an eel," and he recommended usages like "to give assistance" instead of "to assist," and "to make application" instead of "to apply."

Bentham also gave us such classics of later bureaucratese as *maximize, minimize, unilateral,* and *codify.* Today relatively little jargon comes directly from legal language, but vast amounts from the theories of social scientists and bureaucrats trying to modify the law.

"The Language of Artizans"

Scientific and engineering language followed a similar course from trade secret to Tech Speak. Bishop Thomas Sprat's history of the Royal Society of London (1667) described in a famous passage how it had "exacted from all its members, a close, naked, natural way of speaking; positive expressions; clear senses; a native easiness; bringing all things as near the Mathematical plainness, as they can: and preferring the language of Artizans, Countrymen, and Merchants, before that, of Wits, or Scholars."

It turned out that everyday language would not do, either. Another early devotee of science, John Wilkins, published a book the next year that pointed out how ambiguous everyday language really was, "witness those words of *Break, Bring, Cast, Cleare, Come, Cut, Draw, Fall, Hand, Keep, Day, Make, Pass, Put, Run, Set, Stand, Take,* none of which have less than thirty or forty, and some of them about a hundred several senses. . . ."

Wilkins's solution was a system of squiggles, looking like Arabic script, in which each element was supposed to represent one, and only one, thing itself. Of course it remained a curiosity, but Wilkins and other early crusaders for a universal language had made their point. English as it stood, whether flowery or plain, was getting in the way of truth.

The scientific side of Tech Speak began with the dilemmas that early modern scientists faced. They could not use the rhetoric of the courtiers and preachers, yet they also needed something more exact than everyday speech. Linnaeus, the master of Latin classification, was famous for his terse style.

By the nineteenth century, scientific English was so entrenched that attempts to change it seemed more bizarre than any of the actual jargon. The purifiers of English, in trying to rid the language of all foreign roots, fell back on expressions like *earthlore* instead of *geology*, *fireghost* for *electricity*, and *forestoning* for *fossil*.

Today scientists, engineers, and physicians probably use no more technical language than 20 other professions. *Pulsars, quasars, black holes, white dwarfs,* and *quarks* are words that hardly reflect pompous minds. But scientists have retained from the seventeenth century a profound suspicion of eloquent argument. Where lawyers see no injustice in having a case decided for the party with the more articulate champion, scientists believe that evidence, not persuasion, must prevail. Of course, this leads some of them to a kind of reverse rhetoric that uses needless complexity to imply an absence of verbal tricks. Here again, language reform has led to what is denounced as language abuse.

Warspeak

The military uses its own Tech Speak on a scale that rivals even that of lawyers and scientists. It is not just that warfare mixes politics, science, and technology, and borrows from the language of each. It is also that the enemy's speech fascinates the soldier, who comes to believe bits of it can do wonders for his arsenal.

Arsenal is in fact a word that Europeans, beginning with the medieval Venetians, took from their Arab foes. Admirals also bear an originally Arabic title, literally "commander of." The outer fortifications that guarded European cities probably took their name, *barbican,* from an Arabic word meaning "gate with holes."

Centuries later, Joseph Addison could complain in the *Spectator* that "the present War has so adulterated our Tongue with strange Words, that it would be impossible for one of our Great Grandfathers to know what his Posterity have been doing, were he to read their Exploits in a Modern News-Paper." English soldiers were sending "Accounts of their Performances in a Jargon of Phrases, which they learn among their Conquered Enemies."

When America captured German rocket scientists at the end of the Second World War, it unwittingly began an even more fateful process—linguistically, at least. Even before the war, *flak* (*Fliegerabwehrkanone,* or "aviator-defense-gun") was making its way into English. While scientific and technical German remains backward in the use of Latin roots, it has a splendid capacity for stringing together almost endless groups of nouns. Germans often refer to a car as a PKW (*Personenkraftwagen,* or "personal-motor-vehicle") and a truck as an LKW (*Lastkraftwagen* or "cargo-motor-vehicle"). The video recorder of Anglo-Americans is their *Fernsehsendungaufnahmegerät,* or "televised-transmission-recording-apparatus." (A *New York Times* contributor says the Germans are understandably beginning to use the English expression instead.) And in aerospace engineering itself, a propjet engine is a *Propellerturbinenluftstrahltriebwerk,* and the characteristic blade-slap of a helicopter is *Rotor-Wirbel-Wechselwirkungsgeräusch.* It is hard to prove, of course, but very possible that this tendency helped form the aerospace dialect that the sociolinguist David McNeill called Space Speak.

In its original home, Space Speak generates phrases like "the nozzle gas ejection ship attitude control system." But Space Speak does not stop at the military's gates. Its influence has spread until it has become the most important single source of Tech Speak. As early as 1966, McNeill discovered that members of Congress used almost as many long noun compounds in speaking as NASA engineers did in writing.

The old army and navy language, no matter how strange to civilians, was not Tech Speak any more than the mysterious formulas of the Celtic lawyers had been. Tech Speak is not so much for communication among an in-group as for demonstrating something to an out-group. Thus the barely reputable *brig* became a (presumably progressive) navy *Correctional Facility* in the 1970s, only to be restored to its original name in the early 1980s. *Bachelor Officers' Quarters* were changed to *Unaccompanied Officer Personnel Housing* and back. *Human Resources* were once again *people.*

Should we applaud the reversal of jargon, in the armed forces or anywhere else? It's tempting to see its defeat as a triumph for common sense. And often it has been. Some fine print exists to befuddle the unwary. Some crimes have been papered over with doubletalk. But then again, as Orwell should have acknowledged, there was no bureaucratese at a Nuremberg rally. When it blurs distinctions or disrupts our usual patterns of thought, jargon can be a neutral meeting ground for resolving social conflicts.

As Geoffrey Nunberg has pointed out, medical euphemisms, too, can be humane rather than mystifying. Hansen's Disease, Alzheimer's Disease, and Down's Syndrome aren't mere euphemisms for leprosy, senility, and idiocy. They express our hope for prevention and better treatment. The good old days could be verbally brutal, and even the *Quarterly Review of Doublespeak* of the National Council of Teachers of English acknowledges the wisdom of renaming as the Elwyn Institutes what had previously been known as the Pennsylvania Training School for

Idiotic and Feeble-Minded Children.

But then, perhaps *training school* was educationese in its day, and the paths of linguistic purity lead but to the workhouse, the poorhouse, or the madhouse.

HARD-COPY OUTPUT DIRECTORY

To speak Tech, read Tech. Browse the technical press, especially magazines like *Aviation Week* and journals like *Nature* and *Science*, and don't overlook humbler trade journals.

If you want to verify Texpressions for scientific or linguistic accuracy, the best general books are the *Oxford English Dictionary* (for earlier Texpressions), the *Merriam-Webster Unabridged Dictionary*, the *American Heritage Dictionary of the English Language*, *Webster's New World Dictionary*, *Roget's International Thesaurus* (fourth edition; the only suitable thesaurus), and the *Encyclopædia Britannica*.

Of specialized references, the best is the *McGraw-Hill Encyclopedia of Science and Technology*, available at most larger public libraries, together with the *McGraw-Hill Dictionary of Scientific and Technical Terms* (preferable to its shorter forms) and the one-volume *Van Nostrand Encyclopedia of Science and Technology*.

Among subject dictionaries, Joseph A. Angelo, Jr.'s *Dictionary of Space Technology* (New York: Van Nostrand Reinhold, 1982); Adrian V. Stokes's *Concise Encyclopedia of Information Technology* (Englewood Cliffs, N.J.: Prentice-Hall, 1982); John Whittow's *Penguin Dictionary of*

Physical Geography (London and New York: Penguin Books, 1984); and the *Penguin Dictionary of Botany* (London and New York: Penguin Books, 1983) are worth trying. In symbolic matters, there is David Crystal's *A First Dictionary of Linguistics and Phonetics* (London: Andre Deutsch, 1980).

It's hard to compare the merits of chemistry, physics, and biology textbooks for Tech Speak, but Eric Rogers's *Physics for the Enquiring Mind* (Princeton: Princeton University Press, 1960) has some of the best and clearest explanations. I have used the outstanding popular books of Harold McGee, *On Food and Cooking* (New York: Charles Scribner's Sons, 1984); Peter J. Brancazio on *Sport Science* (New York: Simon and Schuster, 1984); J. E. Gordon on *Structures* (London: Penguin Books, 1978, and New York: Da Capo, 1981) and on *The New Science of Strong Materials* (London: Penguin Books, 1983, and Princeton: Princeton University Press, 1984).

Techronym Index

TECHRONYM INDEX